The Strength of a King

A Metaphorical Look at the Attributes and Amenities of a King and His Kingdom

Overseer Terry Mathis Clark Sr.

Foreward by Bishop Randy Borders

Unless otherwise indicated, all scriptures are taken from the King James Version of the Bible

First published by Dog Ear Publishing
4010 W. 86th Street, Ste H
Indianapolis, IN 46268
www.dogearpublishing.net

ISBN: 978-159858-616-9

This book is printed on acid-free paper.

Printed in the United States of America

Dedication

I would like to dedicate this, my first literary work to the person who has been the greatest source of strength to me throughout my adult life. Without whom none of my many accomplishments would not have come to fruition. Since 1985 I have been blessed and honored to call her my wife. She is both friend and lover, the mother of my two wonderful handsome sons. She is the one of the greatest examples of a woman that has successfully stood by her husband and raised her children in the nurture and admonition of the Lord. She has taken care of her home, fulfilled her call in ministry serving as the Minister of Worship in Christ Harvest Church, as well as accomplished her dream of becoming a registered nurse and is currently furthering her education. I am extremely proud to be her husband and am grateful to God for the bone of my bone and the flesh of my flesh. When all else fails and if everyone else leaves, Meshelle has proven that she will always be there to strengthen me, and I know that two are better than one, but these two have become one. I love you dear; you help me do what I do. Thank you.

Terry M. Clark Sr.

Special Thanks and Recognition

There are many people in my life that deserve thanks and recognition; I'd like to mention those that have made the biggest impact. First and foremost my parents, Elder Yvonne Thomas Clark and Mr. Mack Kincaid Clark. Bishop Leonard Randolph Borders, thanks for all your support and encouragement. To my mentor, brother and the spiritual leader of our family, Bishop Eric Kincaid Clark Sr., (my favorite preacher in the whole world!) To one of my spiritual fathers, the one that saw the gift of God in me when I was but a teenager, Bishop Brian Keith Williams, thank you for the impartation. To the memory of the late Rev. Landis Carlton Brown Jr. The Fathers in the Body of Christ that I have admired appreciated and studied. Bishop Jesse Delano Ellis II, Bishop Luther James Blackwell, Apostle Otis Lockette, Bishop H. Eugene Bellinger, Bishop Timothy Clarke, Bishop William Washington, Dr. Jerry Fryer, Bishop George Searight, Apostle Barbara Cameron, Bishop Donald Hilliard II, Bishop Donald Anthony Wright, Bishop Liston Page, Bishop E. Earl Jenkins, Bishop Otis Sneed, and the late Bishop Bill McKinney. To all Harvest Church Ministries Int. Pastors, to my best friend Pastor Jerome Haygood, my covenant brothers, Pastor Darryl L. Grant, Bishop Kenneth M. Yelverton, Apostle Frank M. Chatmon, Bishop Frederick M. Brown, Elder Everett Spencer, my spiritual son, Pastor Robert "Jo Jo" Hill, to my elder brother, Pastor Donnell Albert Clark Sr. the most faithful man I know. To my children Terry Mathis Clark Jr. and Devon Michael Clark, I love you guys and I am proud to be your dad.

Very Special Thanks to some key supporters of this project. Your support and belief in this project has not only inspired and encouraged me, but it has enabled me bring my vision to fruition, thank you all. Antoine and Latonya Lassiter, Kevin and Yolanda Warren, Yvonne Clark, Jonathan and Felicia Carter, Nikyta Warren, Tara Hedgepeth, Charles and Margaret McCloud, Latresia Peak, Precious James, Kimry Taylor, Rosa Cooper, Greg Lassiter, Tiffany Lassiter. Twanna Howard, Annette Johnson, and Pamela Montgomery. Lastly, Christ Harvest Church…**Life to the Family!**

Table of Contents

Foreward

The church, as we know it, has evolved into a state that is far from her initial conception. She (the church) was conceived in eternity, but released in time in a Mediterranean culture. This culture became monarchial in nature, with kings, queens, and their kingdoms. Through imperialism this concept was birthed in Europe and much of the known world, *even America*. Settlers to the new world braved the dangerous journeys, crossing treacherous waters in hopes of finding a better life, but once they got here they felt the need to escape the dictates of the monarchy or the King and Queen. Thus, we had the revolutionary war. We wanted independence from the monarchy and we got it. Yes, America the beautiful was a nation founded upon the escape from monarchial type government and its imperialism.

Here we are now over 200 years removed, with little or no understanding of what a kingdom consist of and how it operates. The scripture says, "first natural, then spiritual." Though we speak of KINGDOM living and KINGDOM authority, the church herself suffers from the inability to relate to God as her sovereign ruler and to the saints as kingdom-citizens. Once again, Terry Clark, in *The Strength of a King,* masterfully handles the subject matter; paralleling for us how an earthly kingdom is similar to the Kingdom of God. He uses a scholarly approach to separate the trivial from the essential, showing us the importance of the biblical references to the kingdom; our need to understand every symbolic inference; and the value of it's' preservation. He answers for us many of the age-old questions that seem to permeate our culture. How does a kingdom operate? How is one chosen to be a leader in the kingdom? What is the real function and responsibility of kingdom leadership? Is there any significant difference between leadership and laity? Is pastoral leadership much overrated?

This book is a must read for every person who wants a deeper understanding of how God views the Body of Christ and its leadership. It is my personal joy to recommend this book and its author to you. For Terry Clark this is more than a sermon message, a treatise, a thesis, or a book…it is a revelation birthed through over 25 years of ministerial experience that is in practice in his personal life. He and his wife, Meshelle, model servant-leadership, respect for authority, and true ministerial integrity. I have had the opportunity to walk close to the two of them over the past five years and I can say that I have never met a couple more committed to their kingdom assignment. As their pastor, they have made my job easier and my ministry stronger. Overseer Clark is more than qualified to take us on the journey that you are about to embark upon in *The Strength of a King*. Put on your seat belt, sit back and enjoy the ride. It's sure to be an "unforgettable experience".

Bishop Randy Borders
Presiding Prelate, *Harvest Church Ministries International*
Senior Pastor, *Faith Harvest Church*

The Strength of a King

Introduction

While there are many analogies used throughout scripture to compare our relationship with God, His Church and His Leaders there are few greater than that of the kingdom and the king. In fact the Bible says that we are Kings and Priests unto our God, in Rev. 1:6 as well as Rev. 5:10 We want to take some time and look at Godly leadership and its parallels to both a natural kingdom and the heavenly kingdom to be established on earth. According to the words of Jesus in Matthew 6:10 we are to pray *"Lord let thy kingdom come thy will be done in earth as it is in heaven" what* exactly did he mean? Is this to be a literal coming of the kingdom? Or is it simply another metaphor, allegory or figurative expression speaking to us only of the hereafter, therefore ultimately unattainable in this life. As you may have surmised the answer to that question is a resounding NO! Christ fully intends for us to experience heaven on earth, but in order for that to take place there are a few things that we need to understand. First and foremost, what is a kingdom? A kingdom is any area or realm of influence where a king has total dominion and where the will of the king goes forth uncontested.

That means that in order to experience heaven on earth the will of the king must go forth without resistance or opposition. However the king that we are referring to includes but is not limited to

God the Father and or the Lord Jesus Christ. Hold your horses, as we explain the plan of God for His kingdom and His Church as we look at and examine the strength of king and how we can see the kingdom of God established in our lives and our local churches and ultimately in the Body of Christ.

Since the beginning of time, whenever God wanted to lead a people, the first thing He did was choose a leader. "Many are called but few are chosen" God doesn't simply call leaders but he chooses them, *Jer 1:5 Before I formed thee in the belly I knew thee; and before thou camest forth out of the womb I sanctified thee, and I ordained thee a prophet unto the nations.* When God sets up a leader it is a sovereign act. He doesn't consult with us, nor does he care about our leadership criteria. In fact most of the leaders that God chose according to scripture would not be qualified by our standards in today's Church. Men like Moses, a murderer. How about Abraham a liar, Jacob a trickster or Judah who had intentionally hired a prostitute, but unknowingly committed incest. Perhaps you'd like to have David as your pastor, as we well know he committed adultery and murder in one act of sin and cover up.

One thing for sure we all have something that in the eyes of man would disqualify us from leadership, aren't you glad that God is sovereign and doesn't need mans approval. God is a God of order and governs His kingdom and His church through delegated authority that is He uses those whom He chooses and demands that we honor and respect His delegates. There is no other way to see the kingdom of God manifested in your life. You must submit yourself to Godly leadership and honor the men and women that He establishes and sets up in the earth. This book is designed to help you properly identify, serve, honor and submit to the God ordained authorities and leadership in your life, whether it be in your home, in the local church or even in your field of profession. As you read this book you will also learn how to flow as a king and priest in your own life. How to exercise your God given authority in the earth. You are a king, which is to say you are royalty, but do you know where your strength really lies?

Let us examine those things that are closely associated with a king or a kingdom, and look at the spiritual application to Godly leadership as well as personal relationships. As we do so we will seek to find practical applications to the biblical principals that we discover.

Chapter One

Anointed, but not Appointed

One of the first and most important things that God will do when choosing someone for service is anoint them. If you've ever been anointed by God to do a work (and if you are reading this, I suspect you have) you know that while receiving the anointing may be an act or single event, producing the anointing is indeed a process.

Most every leader can look back on the day when they were separated for God's service. What a range of emotions everything from joy to fear, from excitement to anxiety, from being nervous to being anxious, humbled and proud all in the same moment. What a great and glorious day. It takes a while for most of us to realize that this is only the beginning of a life long journey filled with all of those same emotions that flooded your heart on that first day, only now the span of time separating one feeling from another seems like an eternity and your anointing seems more like a sentence then a salute. But this is your destiny, you are called and chosen and destined for greatness, only no one told you what the road to greatness looked like. It looks much like the road to destruction and despair, filled with uncertainty and if not for the comfort of the Holy Spirit we would certainly faint, at least in our minds.

In God's infinite wisdom He has charted a course designed specifically for you with the express purpose of producing the anointing in your life. You have gone beyond the answering of the call and now feel the indescribable burden that befalls those that are truly chosen vessels for "many are called but few are chosen" Matthew 22:14 Your process has begun, it doesn't matter whether you are like David our principle character, or many of the other anointed vessels used by God throughout scripture, history and even this present day. Everyone has a process that they have to go through if they are going to see the anointing manifested in their lives.

If we really want to understand our process we must examine the process used for producing the oil used for anointing in the natural. But before we do so there is a concept or principle that I would like to examine. In Exodus chapter 30 there are the instructions given to Moses on how to produce the anointing oil. For everything and everybody that would be used in the service of the Lord and His Tabernacle would have to be anointed. No exceptions and God was very specific about the process of producing the anointing. But before we can appreciate the recipe for the anointing we must understand the importance of following instructions, being obedient. One of the reasons God gave the instructions to Moses is that He could trust Moses to do just what He said. This is very important, to our analogy. Anyone that knows how to cook, well let me rephrase that. "Anyone who has been properly trained in the culinary arts" knows the importance of following the recipe.

The only way to produce a perfect dish on a consistent basis, is to follow the recipe. The only way to insure that the dish is made correctly, is to follow the recipe. The only way to guarantee success when mass distributing a food product, is to follow the recipe! It is one of the most foundational and basic fundamental principles of cooking.

I spent almost twenty years in the restaurant business and in those years of training management teams and opening restaurants all over the nation, one of the hardest things to accomplish on a consistent basis was to make sure that everyone "FOLLWED THE

RECIPE" There was always someone who thought that they could make if better, they would try to add something extra or leave something out, all while trying to produce a product to their liking! Not realizing or considering that the goal of the company was not to produce a product to any one individual's likings, but that recipe had been carefully developed by qualified Chefs who have a much larger perspective. They understand through much research and testing the balance needed in a particular recipe to achieve the desired result. That desired result is determined be the creator of the dish, he has a specific goal, a vision and that is often times much bigger than what we can see or even imagine.

I said all that to say this, God knows what it takes to produce the anointing in your life, your responsibility is to follow God's recipe for your life. Stop trying to add to it, or eliminate the ingredients that we don't particularly care for. He doesn't need our help or our input, we've got to trust that He knows what's best and that He's got our best interest at heart.

I can just imagine that David being left to tend the flock, an outcast from the rest of the family, considered to be the runt of the litter, not even being considered when the prophet Samuel asked to see all of Jesse's sons. While it may have looked like David was forgotten or cast aside, God was gathering the ingredients needed to produce the anointing in David's life. While his brothers were on the battle field, David was fighting the lion and the bear! You, like David may not have the conventional training of your brethren, but you have fought your share of loins and tigers and bears, "Oh My"... the point is that God has trained and equipped you for the work that He has called you to do. Don't be intimidated by those who say that you are not qualified. You just "Follow the Recipe" Now that we are resolved to do it God's way, lets take a look at God's recipe for the anointing oil. *Exodus 30:22-25 Moreover the LORD spake unto Moses, saying, Take thou also unto thee principal spices, of pure myrrh five hundred shekels, and of sweet cinnamon half so much, even two hundred and fifty shekels, and of sweet calamus two hundred and fifty shekels, And of cassia five hundred shekels, after the shekel of the sanctuary, and of oil olive an hin: And thou shalt make it an oil of holy ointment, an ointment compound after the art of the apothecary: it shall be an holy anointing oil.* The first thing that stands out in Exodus 30, are the three things necessary in God's recipe for the anointing.

The Person
The Product
The Process

"Moreover the Lord spake unto Moses" the instructions were given to Moses. This is significant because it suggest that the anointing cannot be produced buy just anyone and it certainly cannot be produced by everyone. God has spoken to someone, a person, a man or woman of God and He has given them the recipe or the word for your life. You won't get it directly from the Lord, you need that chosen person. God then uses that person to gather and identify the product. The Lord required "principle spices" choice, excellent, the best. Which required a trained eye as well as sensitive palate. No ingredient is chosen by accident, but everyone is carefully selected so as to produce the best possible result.

The first ingredient is pure myrrh, a very bitter spice extracted from balsam trees by distilling or drop by drop, because of its pleasant aroma it is used in the production of perfumes and incense. Its taste however is very bitter, but it has a medicinal value, much like an astringent acting as antiseptic and even a stimulant.

Then there is sweet cinnamon, which is produced by grinding the inner bark of any of several tropical tress of the laurel family.

Then sweet calamus, the sweet or sugar cane that comes from scraping the roots of the cane tree. Often used in perfumes as well, rare and costly the clamus reed grows along the streams and river banks. When crushed it has the taste of ginger.

Last is cassia, similar to cinnamon in that it is very fragrant but lacks the sweet taste yet has several uses, it is used in dye and also as a cleaning of purifying agent.

It is interesting to note that of the four principle spices two are sweet and two are bitter. But God required twice as much of the bitter spices as he did of the sweet. Just as only God knows what it takes to produce the symbolic anointing oil, only He knows how to produce the anointing in your life. And most times, that's through many bitter experiences mixed in with the sweet things in life.

I've heard it said and found it to be true, that " your greatest area of deliverance is your greatest area anointing" About fourteen or fifteen years ago my wife and I were going through a rough time in our marriage. I'll never forget my pastor telling me that one day I would have a tremendous ministry to marriages. I just knew he had missed God that time, but I also knew that every prophetic word that he had ever given me had come to pass. However I couldn't see it because my heart was broken and it felt as though it would never change, but it did. That seems like a lifetime ago now, and I guess it is because for the last ten years God has given me a tremendous ministry to marriages. Now I realize why it was necessary for my wife and I to go through the experiences that we had.

Without the pain and bitter experiences in life and marriage we could not possibly empathies with couples that are struggling in their marriage. The bible says that in Heb 4:15 that *"we have not an high priest which cannot be touched with the feeling of our infirmities; but was in all points tempted like as we are, yet without sin."* If Christ had to endure temptation and even suffering in order to identify with us, how much more is our suffering necessary in order to minister to those in similar circumstances? How can you minister to a drug attic if you've never used drugs or reach the alcoholic if you've never struggled with a drinking problem? It's true; we minister not just out of our hurt or pain, but out of our deliverance.

Isolated, the ingredients are of limited use, but when they are properly mixed together they can produce something special, something unique, something only God could have planned.

Which brings us to the process. Just because you have gone through some bitter experiences does not mean that you are anointed to minister in that area. It takes the blending of the bitter and the sweet. It was not coming through the bad times in my marriage that qualified me for ministry. It's that, mixed with the wonderful marriage that we have in spite of the bitter times, "that didn't make us bitter." While the anointing is being produced in your life, except both the bitter and the sweet and let God produce the right mix and that will result in an anointing that will touch and change lives while propelling you to your destiny.

The last ingredient is the oil itself. It's important to understand that experience alone is not anointing, you must have the oil. The oil is the spirit of God, and it's the spirit that brings life. The oil comes from the crushing of the olive. Many times we feel like we are being crushed by the pressures and circumstances of our lives. Only God knows how to turn our misery into ministry, our sorrow into service and our problems into purpose. Understanding and accepting your process is an important part of seeing the anointing manifested in your life. Many times we are so anxious to be appointed that we prematurely leave our place of anointing or our process. While David was anointed by the Prophet Samuel in his father's house, David remained in his father's house until God moved him to the next level. It's important that we don't run out as soon as were anointed looking for our place of appointment. While you are going through your anointing process your place of appointment is being prepared for your arrival. Patience and faith in God are essential to your process of being fruitful. Many have forfeited their blessing because they would not wait on God and His timing.

"Isolated *ingredients are of limited use, but when they are properly mixed together they can produce something special, something unique, something only God could have planned, the anointing"*

Chapter Two

Crowned King

We can readily identify royalty by any number of things only attributed to those of such nobility. One of which is the crown that speaks to us of the king's glory and honor. *2 Sam 12:29-30 says and David gathered all the people together, and went to Rabbah, and fought against it, and took it. 30 And he took their king's crown from off his head, the weight whereof was a talent of gold with the precious stones: and it was set on David's head. And he brought forth the spoil of the city in great abundance.* The official act of the stripping of a king's honor is demonstrated by King David as he takes the city of Rabbah, captures its king and utterly humiliates him in the sight of all the people. It is important to guard against those who would seek to take the honor and glory that belongs to the head. The scripture says in *Isa 42:8 I am the LORD: that is my name: and my glory will I not give to another, neither my praise to graven images.* While there is a glory that belongs to God and that glory he will not share or give to another, a great example of this is found in *Acts 12:21-23 "And upon a set day Herod, arrayed in royal apparel, sat upon his throne, and made an oration unto them. And the people gave a shout, saying, It is the voice of a god, and not of a man. 23 And immediately the angel of the Lord smote him, because he gave not God the glory: and he was eaten of worms, and gave up the ghost."* God has no problem with a man receiving honor or glory to a certain extent, that extent not extending to the glory and honor that should only be attributed to God as our source and creator. Ultimately God uses men and it is up to those men to properly direct the people and the praise back to God. That being said lets talk about the crown and what it represents in the life of the believer and the kingdom of God.

The Crown is the head dressing for the king, it is one of the things that separates him from the rest of the people. When we speak of the head dressing we will be speaking metaphorically of the local church and the set gift. We understand that the pastor or set gift, depending on your senior pastor's gifting in particular, is the head of the local church. This must be clearly understood for the church to function according as God has purposed it. There can only be one head, I repeat! There can only be one head, I've heard it said "That anything with two heads is a monster or a freak" Even as the universal body of Christ has a head (*Col 1:18 And he is the head of the body, the church*) so does the local assembly. *Jer 3:15 And I will give you pastors according to mine heart, which shall feed you with knowledge and understanding.* The body can do nothing apart from the head, and it is in the entire body's best interest to take care of its head. Many times the local church would rather see its leaders wearing helmet's than wearing crowns.

We seem to prefer our leaders in a position of warfare rather than a position of royalty. It is this mentality that keeps the kingdom of God from being fully established in the earth. In the scripture it is made abundantly clear that the king must be protected from battle, for he is the visionary. The body can survive with a wound to the hand, the arm or even its figurative legs. I even dare say that the body can survive the amputation of any of these limbs, but the head! Well a severe wound or blow to the head can cripple the entire body and amputation spells its ultimate demise. It is sad that most believers don't see their leader in this very vital role. That is precisely why many Christians find it so easy to just change their church affiliation with no thought of what they are doing to the body. But when we understand Godly leadership and delegated authority in the local church, we will recognize that the presence of Godly leaders represents Christ in the Church and their absence also denotes his absence.

Once the need and desire for God ordained headship has been established, we can proceed to properly adorn the head with a crown befitting the royal priesthood that he or she represents. Jesus said in Luke 16:8 that the children of this world are in their generation wiser than the children of light. Before I am accused of taking this scripture out of context, may I submit to you that this passage not only speaks to us of a literal and spiritual truth, but it also points to some conceptual truths.

One most notable, is that the world knows how to treat its own, in particular its leaders. The world wants its leaders to be free from burden and stress. To enjoy life to the fullest, to live in the best, wear the best and drive the best without fear of persecution from within its own ranks. The world understands that for a leader to be at peak performance it is necessary to remove all distractions. Alleviate all stress and create an environment conducive for visionary growth, development and expansion. To the contrary most churches expect its pastor to be encumbered with burden and the day to day operations of the ministry.

When the apostles were faced with similar problems their solution was simple, *Acts 6:3-4 Look ye out among you seven men of honest report, full of the Holy Ghost and wisdom, whom we may appoint over this business. But we will give ourselves continually to prayer, and to the ministry of the word.* That is the key to successful leadership in the Church. The leader must be in a position to seek the Lord as well as hear from Him at anytime. I for one am not an advocate of pastors working secular jobs. Being a Sr. Pastor of a young church (less than five years old) I am often asked "If I work? Or am I full time" Although I understand the premise of the question, I take issue with its implied notion that pastoring full time or part time is not work. Although there have been times in my pastoral tenure that I have supplemented my income by working a secular job as well as my full time job as pastor. By the way, last I heard we call that working two jobs! However, during those times I found it extremely difficult to be as effective, and productive in ministry. According to *1 Cor*

9:14 Even so hath the Lord ordained that they which preach the gospel should live of the gospel. There were times when men of God in the scripture worked quote unquote secular jobs, for instance in *Neh 13:10-11 I perceived that the portions of the Levites had not been given them: for the Levites and the singers, that did the work, were fled every one to his field. Then contended I with the rulers, and said, Why is the house of God forsaken? And I gathered them together, and set them in their place.* Notice the prophet's question, "why is the house of God forsaken?" The priest had to return to the fields because the people after returning from Babylonian captivity had not resumed the tithing principle. Therefore the prophet had to set things back in order by commanding that the people return to tithing. However, the tithe is what is required. You really have not properly honored your leader until you go above and beyond what is required. Their should be no greater pleasure for believers than to see their leaders blessed and prosperous.

We must understand the principle. What is put on the head will flow down to the rest of the body. Therefore we should not begrudge the crowning of our leaders, but in fact we should embrace it and celebrate it! When we learn to both figuratively and literally crown our leaders, the body will begin to experience the kingdom abundance and blessings that God has designed for His people.

I must caution every leader, not to mistake the anointing process for the official act of being crowned. The anointing, which represents God's calling and separation of a leader, may come many years before the actual manifestation of the promotion that comes when a leader is crowned. Many legitimate God ordained leaders have become frustrated and even discouraged because they failed to realize God's timing in their lives. We have countless examples of God anointing a person for leadership and many years passing before the manifestation of that promise.

Most notable is David being anointed king as a young boy, and not being crowned king for some seventeen years later. The crowning of a king is more a process than an event. As long as we are willing to go through our process, our eventual crowning is inevitable. Don't allow frustration and discouragement to get you off your course or out of your process. Enjoy your victories, your goliath moments, your battles won. But know there will be times when those that once sang your praises may one day in a moment of distress consider stoning you. You must learn to take the good with the bad, the bitter with the sweet. It is at those times that like David you must encourage your self in the Lord, for the scripture says in *James 1:12 "Blessed is the man that endureth temptation: for when he is tried, he shall receive the crown of life"* While the crowning represents the end of one process it also signifies the beginning of another.

Chapter Three

A Kings Throne, the seat of Power

Once crowned the king is officially inaugurated into this royal and prestigious position of power and responsibility. Already crowned with glory and honor the king must now live up to his exalted status by establishing the throne, which is known as the seat of power. The place from which all orders are given, all authority and all power is displayed. The most coveted as well as the most burdensome seat in the entire kingdom.

God has always intended for us to have power in the earth, *Gen 1:26 And God said, Let us make man in our image, after our likeness: and let them have dominion...*You were created to have power, to have dominion to be a king in the earth. *Gen 2:15 And the LORD God took the man, and put him into the garden of Eden to dress it and to keep it.* It is impossible for us to assume our rightful place in the kingdom as well as in the earth if we don't understand the authority that God has given us. Were there is no submission there can be no legitimate authority. One of the biggest problems in the Christian community today, is there are so many in positions of authority, and yet they are not submitted to credible and legitimate authority themselves.

When Jesus was approached by the elders of the Jews as well as the friends of the centurion and eventually the centurion himself. His response was like no other seen in scripture. What was it about this man that so impressed Jesus?

Luke 7:8-9 For I also am a man set under authority, having under me soldiers, and I say unto one, Go, and he goeth; and to another, Come, and he cometh; and to my servant, Do this, and he doeth it. When Jesus heard these things, he marvelled at him, and turned him about, and said unto the people that followed him, I say unto you, I have not found so great faith, no, not in Israel. Jesus obviously was not simply impressed with the centurions position or status in life,. Neither was it his willingness to except the spoken word of Christ. It was not the care that he had shown for his servant, not even his apparent influence over the Jewish leaders. The thing that so greatly impressed Jesus was his understanding of spiritual authority! When you closely look at Jesus' ministry you will find that the greatest source of controversy and contention amongst the leaders of his day was not based on his ability, or his popularity nor understanding of the law, but where did his authority come from?

Mark 1:26-28 And when the unclean spirit had torn him, and cried with a loud voice, he came out of him. 27 And they were all amazed, insomuch that they questioned among themselves, saying, What thing is this? What new doctrine is this? For with authority commandeth he even the unclean spirits, and they do obey him. And immediately his fame spread abroad throughout all the region round about Galilee.

Matt 21:23-24 And when he was come into the temple, the chief priests and the elders of the people came unto him as he was teaching, and said, By what authority doest thou these things? And who gave thee this authority? 24 And Jesus answered and said unto them, I also will ask you one thing, which if ye tell me, I in like wise will tell you by what authority I do these things. From the beginning of His ministry to nearly the end of His earthly ministry the question was asked, "where does His authority come from." All the while he answered over and over again.

John 8:38 I speak that which I have seen with my Father:

John 10:32 Jesus answered them, Many good works have I shewed you from my Father;

John 5:17 Jesus answered them, My Father worketh hitherto, and I work.

Luke 10:22 All things are delivered to me of my Father: and no man knoweth who the Son is, but the Father; and who the Father is, but the Son, and he to whom the Son will reveal him.

If I were to list all the times Jesus revealed the source of His authority, I would have an entire book on this single subject and would not have wasted any of your time! That same authority that Jesus received from the Father He bestowed upon the Church and its leaders! This power or authority is what is called "delegated authority." Which means that the authority ultimately belongs to another, one of higher rank or position. Such authority is conditionally lent to those appointed by said person, a power of attorney if you will. A legal right to act on behalf of another, in this case the Lord God Himself. In every area of life there are authorities set up to govern, execute judgment and hold us accountable. It is amazing how easy it is for us to except and even embrace these authorities in almost every arena. Except when it comes to the Church! We accept the sovereignty of our employer to promote whom ever he sees fit. We submit to the authority delegated to those appointed by our employer. Many Christians fail to discern the importance of being fully submitted to the authority that God has placed in their lives.

When I speak of the seat of power, it is simply a metaphor for identifying a position of authority whether it be in the Church or in your personal life. It is important to recognize those who operate in the Lords name in our lives. There are tremendous benefits and blessings to understanding this simple key. The scripture says "If you receive a prophet in the name of a prophet, you will receive a prophets reward." Which is to say that when you recognize the authority of the prophet or delegated authority of God, then you will receive the same reward of that ministry gift even though you don't carry that burden of ministry. Wow! What a deal! You mean by receiving and properly honoring God ordained leadership, I can have the blessings and rewards that go along with leading God's people released in my life? Even though I'm not a preacher or a prophet? Exactly! According to *2 Chron 20:20 If you "Believe in the LORD your God, so shall ye be established; believe his prophets, so shall ye prosper."* Which means that it is not enough to believe God. You've got to believe those whom God has placed in the seat of power in your life. Everyone should have someone that has authority in their life. Someone that can help them stay on course, stay focused if you will. While many rush to establish their throne or seat of power it is equally important to balance power and authority with accountability.

I would suggest that a good criteria for submitting to a spiritual leader is, examine their level of submission to authority. Are they in fact asking you to do what they themselves are unwilling to do? While there are different levels of submission, everyone should be submitted on some minimal level. While I truly believe that every pastor should have a pastor, I also understand that every situation is unique and while some pastors may be without pastoral covering, everyone needs spiritual connection. What I mean is that "no man is an island" and neither should any ministry be an island.

I feel that there should be at least three components to God ordained pastoral submission. First there should be a connection, this is vital to any relationship whether you are the shepherd or the sheep. Make Godly connections in your life, because the connections you make determine the directions you take. Many well intentioned, God fearing believers have been lead astray as a result of an ungodly connection.

I The Connection

A Godly connection is that unique and often times unexplainable feeling you get when you know that it is more than a casual acquaintance or a fleshly connection. It's a feeling that can't be described with words, you just know! It's like my relationship with my wife. I know that she is the only woman for me. There are plenty of attractive, intelligent women out there but they are not the woman for me. It's not because my wife is perfect, it's because she is perfect for me. It's not because she is the most beautiful, but she is the most beautiful to me, or the most intelligent, well you get the picture. Many times we fail to make our Godly connections because we are looking for perfection in imperfect beings through imperfect eyes. One of the reasons I know that my wife is the perfect woman for me is because I know how flawed I am, and so does she and she loves me anyway. We are connected and no one can sever that connection, "what God has joined together let no man put asunder" That is the same way you should feel about your connection to your leader, you may not be able to describe it in words, but you know in your heart that God has connected you to your leader and you are not going to allow anything or anyone to separate you from your leader. Just as Peter replied to Jesus when asked, *Will ye also go away? Then Simon Peter answered him, Lord, to whom shall we go? Thou hast the words of eternal life. And we believe and are sure that thou art that Christ, the Son of the living God. John 6:67-69 KJV.* While there are many qualified leaders in the world today, there is only one ordained for you. You must value and protect that connection.

The connections you make in life will make or break you. I once heard *Bishop Eric Clark* say "if you want to destroy someone, just put a fool in their life" for the bible says in *Proverbs 13:20 He that walketh with wise men shall be wise: but a companion of fools shall be destroyed.* Therefore it behooves all of us to be very prayerful about how we choose our connections, for instance our spouse, our vocation and especially our spiritual covering. Which brings me to number two.

II The Covering

There should be covering. You might ask what is the difference between connection and covering? Connection speaks of our being joined, kind of like marriage that's why the bible say's "be not unequally yoked with unbelievers." Because once you become joined God seals the union. You don't want to be joined to someone that is not going in the same direction that you are going, or doesn't believe the same things as you believe. The prophet Amos asks the question "can two walk together except they agree? Of course this is a rhetorical question, the implied answer is no! So before you get married, join a church or even chose a career. Make sure that you have a common vision and goals that are compatible so that your connection won't adversely affect your direction. Covering on the other hand speaks directly to the spiritual authority a leader has in your life with God and man and most importantly, with you.

It's like the protection you have with an insurance agency. If you have an accident you don't have to worry as long as you have adequate coverage. In the marriage the husband is the God ordained covering, or the protector of the family. He stands before God on behalf of the family. In the church the covering is the pastor or set gift.

It feels much more comforting when I am driving my automobile knowing that I am covered by one of the most reputable insurance companies in the business. However it doesn't cause me to become careless or reckless, just comforted to know that I'm not out there by myself. I've got someone in authority backing me up, even though I can't see them they are there. And as long as I keep my part of the contract, I have nothing to fear. I'm covered! Well I'm not just covered by my insurance company, but I have a spiritual covering that has not only the ability but the authority to act on my behalf. As a Pastor I have found that many people seek a connection without covering. In other words they want a relationship without responsibility, accessibility without accountability. They want you to be their

Preacher but not their Pastor. But to have a covering means to be under someone, to be submitted as I referred to earlier in the chapter *Luke 7:8-9 For I also am a man set under authority.* I have a covering, this should be the testimony of every leader as well as every believer. Don't settle for a connection without covering. When you connect with a leader, submit to their covering so that you can reap all the benefits that flow from the seat of power. Once you've made your connection, submitted to covering, there should be a covenant.

III The Covenant

Many people make the connection, some even submit to covering, but very few actually understand covenant. The covenant is the most important part of our relationship with God, our leaders and each other. Without it our connection can be easily severed and our covering rendered ineffective. The covenant is the third of that three fold cord in relationship, you know, *Eccl 4:12 "A threefold cord is not quickly broken."*

Unfortunately most of us have never been taught the importance of covenant relationship. We live in such a litigious society that contractual agreements supersede covenantal relationships. The difference between a contract and a covenant is monumental and warrants some scrutiny in the context of our story. A contract is an agreement between two or more parties in which each party seeks to protect his own rights or interest. Clauses and other amendments may be added in order to penalize the opposing party in the event of breach or infraction thereby releasing the offended party from obligation. In other words in a contractual agreement we only look out for ourselves! We are in it to get the most out of it while giving as little as possible. Where as a covenant is an agreement between two or more parties in which each party seeks to protect the interest and rights of one another. Committing to fulfill his vow irregardless of the actions of the other parties. The agreement is not contingent or conditional.

In other words in a covenant we look out for one another! For too many of us this is like speaking a foreign language, to actually prefer someone else's interest above our own, why that is absurd, ridiculous, just plain foolish, right??? Wrong!

God is a covenant keeping God, He honors covenant and it is through covenant that He intends to bless us and bring us into relationship and prosperity and ultimately our destinies. *Ex 24:8 Behold the blood of the covenant,*

Gen 6:18 But with thee will I establish my covenant;

Gen 15:18 In the same day the LORD made a covenant with Abram,

Ex 6:5 I have remembered my covenant.

2 Chron 21:7 Howbeit the LORD would not destroy the house of David, because of the covenant that he had made with David

In biblical times covenant was understood and expected in relationship, friendship and companionship (family, friends and marriage) but the greatest covenant of all is our covenant with God and our spiritual leader. David understood covenant as exemplified in his covenant with Jonathan. *1 Sam 18:3 Then Jonathan and David made a covenant, because he loved him as his own soul.* The covenant should not be one sided, the thing that allows us to give ourselves freely and completely without fear is that we trust that our covenant partner is doing the same for us. When you commit to follow a leader you must trust that as you give your all, that your leader is likewise giving their all to protect and guide you in the path of righteousness. When it comes to trusting each other many of us have deep reservations based on everything from past bad experiences to personal insecurities. Until we learn to establish, honor and respect covenant relationship it is impossible for us to comprehend Gods kingdom and how it functions.

Connection, Covering and Covenant, when all three components are properly functioning in our relationships we are positioned to experience kingdom manifestation in every area of our lives and ministries. The throne cannot be established without them.

"King Solomon passed all the kings of the earth in riches and wisdom."
—2 Chron. ix. 22.

The Throne. The Seat of Power"

Chapter 4

The Signet Ring

As we further explore and examine the articles associated with royalty we must carefully consider the significance of the ring, in particular the signet ring. It is also important to understand that rings denote relationship. The presence of a ring is the sign that one is betrothed to another. It is the ring that makes the announcement long before words are exchanged in a conversation. When perusing a room for a potential mate or date, one first looks for the quintessential and even universal sign of eligibility, " The ring finger" if present, the would be pursuer quickly moves on to the next potential target. But when absent the eager and now inspired suitor sees opportunity and must now seek to execute his strategy with hopes of success and perhaps bestow a ring of promise and covenant upon the available beauty himself. However the ring does not exclusively denote relationship. There is a ring, the signet ring that not only embodies the essence of relationship but speaks to us of so much more. Long before the days of picture IDs and finger prints, voice recognition and even retina scans and let's not forget DNA analysis. One of the most popular forms of identification was the signet. Of course in those days identity theft was not as big a problem as it is today, seeing that the penalty for such behavior was extremely severe and could result in the death of the perpetrator!

Identity, Authority and Immutability.

Throughout history kings and governing authorities have made signet rings to proclaim their identity, signify authority, and validate their official documents declaring their laws, judgments and commandments.

In Gen 38 the story is told of Judah and his daughter in law:16-18 And she said, What wilt thou give me, that thou mayest come in unto me?17 And he said, I will send thee a kid from the flock. And she said, Wilt thou give me a pledge, till thou send it?18 And he said, What pledge shall I give thee? And she said, **Thy signet**, and thy bracelets, and thy staff that is in thine hand. And he gave it her, and came in unto her, and she conceived by him...24-26 And it came to pass about three months after, that it was told Judah, saying, Tamar thy daughter in law hath played the harlot; and also, behold, she is with child by whoredom. And Judah said, Bring her forth, and let her be burnt.25 When she was brought forth, she sent to her father in law, saying, By the man, whose these are, am I with child: and she said, Discern, I pray thee, whose are these, the signet, and bracelets, and staff.26 And Judah acknowledged them, and said, She hath been more righteous than I; because that I gave her not to Shelah my son. And he knew her again no more. Before we can consider authority or immutability, identity must be established. Judah's identity was established by his signet ring. Like Judah God has put his signet on us and even at our lowest point we cannot deny who we are. Once his identity was established he had to except responsibility for his actions, which would affect his family for generations to come. Though he appears to exhibit true repentance, he is not released from the consequences of his actions.

According to *Deut 23:2 A bastard shall not enter into the congregation of the LORD; even to his tenth generation shall he not enter into the congregation of the LORD.* While this may seem cruel and unjust to us, God placed such high value on the Father that He made it a prerequisite to enter into the congregation of the LORD, or in or modern vernacular, to join the Church. No wonder David said I was glad when they said unto me, Let us go into the house of the LORD. In order to identify with your heavenly father you had to be able to identify with your earthly father for at least ten generations and David was the tenth generation from Judas sin. It is the father that gives us our identity. You have your fathers name. Some may say no sir I have my mothers name! May I submit to you that all names are taken from the father and even if you have your mother's name, that is the name of her father. There is no name in the earth that is traced back to the origin of the mother.

Therefore our identity is found in our father, and that's why God describes Himself as *"A father of the fatherless" Ps 68:5* Contrary to popular belief God never said that He would be a mother to the motherless! But the fatherless, those who have no identity He claims as His own and makes provision for them and gives them a new name. Jesus says in *Matt 23:9 And call no man your father upon the earth: for one is your Father, which is in heaven.* He is teaching us a principle, which is not to limit our origin or identity to our earthly father. While He honored His father and His mother on the earth when it came to His identity, authority and ability He constantly deferred to His heavenly father. For instance in *John 5:43 He said "I am come in my Father's name, and ye receive me not: if another shall come in his own name, him ye will receive".*

As well as in John 8:18-19 I am one that bear witness of myself, and the Father that sent me beareth witness of me. 19 Then said they unto him, Where is thy Father? Jesus answered, Ye neither know me, nor my Father: if ye had known me, ye should have known my Father. also. They were trying to limit His identity to His earthly father, which in doing so would have limited His authority in the earth. Encompassed in the signet would be the family crest amongst other important symbols and inscriptions. This portion was to establish identity therefore determining levels of privilege and authority as well economic status. It doesn't really matter whether or not you were raised by your father or if you've never laid eyes on him before. Trying to find your identity in your earthly father will only limit your authority and ability in the kingdom and in the earth. Many cannot receive from their heavenly father because they have so many "Daddy issues" so they spend their entire life searching for identity.

Going from church to church even looking for a spiritual father but never being able to submit to or receive one because of all the unresolved issues that we have with our natural fathers. I realize however that everyone does not fall into this category. There are many who have great relationships with both their natural and spiritual fathers. For those identity should not be an issue, but do you understand the authority as well as rights and privileges that are afforded to you because of who your father is? Don't ever make the mistake of thinking it's because of who you are. If you do, you may find yourself making the mistake of one biblically infamous son..

His story can be found in *Luke 15:11-32 A certain man had two sons: And the younger of them said to his father, Father, give me the portion of goods that falleth to me. And he divided unto them his living.* We all know the story of the prodigal son. His problem was that he sought to establish his own identity. Like many of us we take the blessings of God and try to do our own thing, only to find ourselves searching for true happiness all the while waddling in life's many pigs' pins. But when he came to himself, he remembered his father and upon his return it was his father who was waiting all along. While there are many lessons in this parable, I want to take special note of the fact that the father through a party, killed the fatted calf, put a robe on his back and "a ring on his finger." Identity, authority and immutability. It wasn't until he remembered who his father was that he came to himself, and his father put a ring on his finger so that he would never forget again. God wants to give you a signet ring. A continual reminder of who He is therefore establishing who you are. Find your identity in Him, release your past and forgive your fathers both natural and spiritual and watch your heavenly Father do exceeding abundantly above what you can think or ask.

The signet also is a symbol of authority. While some rings are simply designed to beautify and accent, and even to denote relationship this ring is so much more that just a piece of jewelry. Along with establishing identity the signet was used to seal official documents and letters, it was the seal that authenticated and made official any decrees or ordinances set forth by the king.

In the book of Esther we see how important the signet ring is in the kingdom. When the decree was made to kill all the Jews it could not be reversed because it had been sealed with the king's ring. But God gave Esther favor with the king and the king in return gave Ester permission to use his signet ring. *Esther 8:7-8 Then the king Ahasuerus said unto Esther the queen and to Mordecai the Jew, Behold, I have given Esther the house of Haman, and him they have hanged upon the gallows, because he laid his hand upon the Jews. 8 Write ye also for the Jews, as it liketh you, in the king's name, and seal it with the king's ring: for the writing which is written in the king's name, and sealed with the king's ring, may no man reverse.* Though the enemy wants to destroy you and has even decreed that you are defeated, you my friend have favor with the King! But not just any king, the King of kings and He has given you permission to use His signet ring. That's right, once you've established your identity in him he gives you authority to use his name.

John 14:14 If ye shall ask any thing in my name, I will do it.

John 16:23 Whatsoever ye shall ask the Father in my name, he will give it you.

Matt 18:18 Verily I say unto you, Whatsoever ye shall bind on earth shall be bound in heaven: and whatsoever ye shall loose on earth shall be loosed in heaven.

It is important however to note that the authority that we are given to use the name of Jesus is not a blank check or cart blanc if you will to do whatever we want. God is not our puppet, gene or good luck charm. Jesus clearly gave the pattern for us to use his name. He was our example and he said...*John 8:28-29 When ye have lifted up the Son of man, then shall ye know that I am he, and that I do nothing of myself; but as my Father hath taught me, I speak these things. 29And he that sent me is with me: the Father hath not left me alone; for I do always those things that please him.* So when Jesus tells us to ask in His name, we are to do and ask those things that please Him.

It literally means to ask as His agent or as His representative. Therefore we cannot ask in His name until we have discovered His will. Upon doing so we can ask what we will and it shall be done. We have authority in Jesus' name to act as His agent and execute His will in the earth.

When the body fully understands this principle then we become effective in establishing the kingdom of God in the earth. Blessings and prosperity are good, but that's not why he gave us authority to use His name! He said *"These signs shall follow them that believe;* **In my name** *shall they cast out devils; they shall speak with new tongues; They shall take up serpents; and if they drink any deadly thing, it shall not hurt them; they shall lay hands on the sick, and they shall recover" Mark 16:17-18* Let's not take the name of the LORD in vain; *"For the LORD will not hold him guiltless that taketh his name in vain".* Exodus 20:7

"When Jesus tells us to ask in His name it literally means to ask as His agent or as his representative".

Chapter 5

The Robes

One of, if not the most notable signs of royalty would certainly be his or her wardrobe. The attire has been a visible sign of success, prominence, stature and nobility since the beginning of recorded history. Even today one is often judged by his attire. Whether in the business world the fashion industry, entertainment and certainly in the church! Why are we seemingly so obsessed with fashion, how we look and what we wear. Well before we get all spiritual and call everyone with fashion sense carnal or queer lets take a look at the origin. The beginning if you will of fashion *(for lack of a better word)* lets look at its purpose and significance. I think once we get a little understanding, we can have a greater appreciation for the principal and purpose of the both the royal and well as liturgical attire. *Exodus 28:1-4 And take thou unto thee Aaron thy brother, and his sons with him, from among the children of Israel, that he may minister unto me in the priest's office, even Aaron, Nadab and Abihu, Eleazar and Ithamar, Aaron's sons.2 And thou shalt make holy garments for Aaron thy brother for glory and for beauty.3 And thou shalt speak unto all that are wise hearted, whom I have filled with the spirit of wisdom, that they may make Aaron's garments to consecrate him, that he may minister unto me in the priest's office.4 And these are the garments which they shall make; a breastplate, and an ephod, and a robe, and a broidered coat, a mitre, and a girdle: and they shall make holy garments for Aaron thy brother, and his sons, that he may minister unto me in the priest's office.*

The first thing we notice in this passage of scripture is that the wearing of robes and special garments for the priest and those that would minister in the tabernacle and in the Holy things was instituted by God. This was not some plot hatched by leaders designed to exalt themselves and separate themselves from the people. This was God's plan and he gave this command to Moses and without hesitation Moses and the people obeyed. With that said I think it is very important that a leader looks like a leader for a number of reasons. First and foremost it is obvious that it is important to God. Why is it important to God? The number one reason may be, the leader represents God to the people. When God called Moses to be his representative, Moses was filled with excuses and yet he was the one God chose. God quickly answers all questions and confirms with signs that He had indeed chosen Moses. However Moses still felt inadequate for the task therefore God gave Moses Aaron to be his helper or spokesmen if you will. And this is what God said.. *Exodus 4:16 And he shall be thy spokesman unto the people: and he shall be, even he shall be to thee instead of a mouth, **and thou shalt be to him instead of God.*** In other words, God said even though I will give you help, you must represent me to the people. Including those that are called to help you in ministry "***and thou shalt be to him instead of God".***

The robes were given for beauty and for glory. Every article in the priest garments had specific meaning and value and when properly understood represented the glory of God. When you read Exodus twenty eight the entire chapter is given to the making and purpose of the priestly garments. I would encourage you to read this chapter and realize that when we properly discern and reverence the things of God we will see a greater manifestation of Gods presence in our lives and our churches. The robes of the priest, the bishop or even the pastor are not simply religious garments, but when worn properly with understanding and reverence speak to us of Royalty, Rank and Relationship. The kingly and priestly garments were specially designed for the office. There were no nock off kingly garments or bargain basement priestly look alikes, to wear them was to be honored and excepted at the highest levels of spiritual and governmental authority. *Psalm 132:9 Let thy priests be clothed with righteousness; and let thy saints shout for joy.* It wasn't until recent years that I came to understand and appreciate the vestments of the priesthood. Oh sure I did what most of the other elders and clergy did on the first Sunday of each month, at funerals and other official occasions. I reluctantly put on my uncomfortable and unfashionable civic attire and performed my religious duty. One day I felt compelled to research the history of vestments and clergy attire, only to be convicted in my spirit for my ignorance, lack of respect and overall irreverence concerning these Holy garments that I have been privileged to adorn by virtue of the call and anointing that God by His sovereign grace and mercy had conferred upon me.

Being an overseer in the Lords church and a member of the African American Joint College of Pentecostal Bishops, I now understand not only the purpose of the robes, but the symbolism for which each article represents. While it may serve little purpose to explain the specific purpose of each article in the levitical priesthood found in Exodus twenty eight. I certainly can see the value of a brief description and explanation of the current day vestments of the clergy. All definitions and explanations taken from **"The Adjutant's guide to Etiquette" by Bishop Randy Borders.**

"THE VESTMENTS"

Chasuble – The chasuble developed from the cloak of the worker (casual), who needed it for protection for the elements. The farmer could work the fields while it was raining, as he could look down inside the front of his casual to see what he was doing. By the 3rd century, the casual was worn by all Christians, but by decrees of Emperor Alexander Severus it was restricted from women. At this same time, the Church restricted it further to only clergy. **It is the symbol of waiters at the table of the Lord. It symbolizes the yoke of Christ and signifies charity. It symbolizes the covering of Noah's nakedness.**

Stole – It symbolizes the clerical office and the yoke of Christ. It is the yoke of the preacher.

Cope - Shepherd's outdoor garment. It symbolizes the Shepherd's covering of the sheep from its nakedness and exposure.

Cassock (tunic) – The mark of the Servant/Scholar – It is the close-fitting garment and may be worn by all ordained clergy as a symbol of a servant. It is the central vestment of the priesthood. It is floor-length, with 33 buttons total (representing Christ's earthly years), topped with a Roman collar. The Bishop continues to wear the cassock as part of his garb because Jesus instructed that those who would be chief among us must be a servant.

Surplice – The surplice, like the rochet, is a knee-length, white vestment worn over the choir cassock, but by elders, priests/pastors, deacons, and seminarians rather than bishops. It is typically simple in design, but can be very fancy. It is distinct from the rochet not in the level of decoration, but in the sleeve: the sleeve, like an alb, fits flush against the choir cassock; the sleeve of a surplice is fuller, and often bell-shaped. **It is the liturgical garment worn by all clergy, used in processions, and when administering the Sacrament. It is the symbol of the priesthood – the ephod for Samuel.**

Rochet – The sign of the Celebrant/Priest. It is a ceremonial garment similar to the surplice but only worn by Bishops. It is symbolic of Aaron's white linen ephod, found in the Book of Leviticus. The white rocket, worn by the Bishop and white surplice worn by the Elders is a symbol of the wearer's role as celebrant of the Sacraments and Chief Worship Leader among the people.

Chimere – The Prophet's mantle/The Preacher's Coat. This garment serves as a symbol of the mantle of a prophet. The chimere is only worn by the Bishop because it signifies him as chief proclaimer and defender of the faith in the Apostolic tradition.

Tippet/Bishop's Scarf – Like the stole it is a symbol of the preacher and one who is yoked. It is larger than the stole.

Pontiff Collar/Neckband shirt – The Slaves dog insignia – ministers were beheaded in the past for their stand in Christianity. Christian ambassadors would place a metal plate around their necks and cover it with white cloth; therefore, making it difficult to behead the Christian soldier.

Rabat – This is worn as the habit of the priest. Ordained elders and bishops wear this attire. The Rabat is worn with a black suit with pontiff collar or neckband shirt. This is also known as his civic attire.

Cincture – Symbol of the Servant to mankind – Material formed in a cummerbund-like style with the cassock and girded the waist, serves as the symbol of humility. The Scriptures tells us that we must be girded with truth and one such truth is that the minister is first and foremost a humble servant. It obtained its symmetry from the towel which our Lord girded Himself with, as He humbled Himself to wash His disciples feet.

Mitre – The crown of the Prince/The Holy Ghost – The liturgical headdress is worn by Popes, Cardinals, and Bishops. The points symbolize the cloven tongue on the heads of the disciples on the day of Pentecost and the streamers represent the everlasting living water that Christ offers to the believer.

Zuchetto/Skull cap – Bishop's indoor covering.

The Appointments:

Gold Chain and Cross – The Royal Servant with a Message- The gold chain is also a symbol of endurance which emphasizes that the bearer is not a novice. The gold represents wealth. As a gift to the Christ Child it symbolizes kingship. Bishops, only, shall wear the gold chain with the Pectoral Cross.

Ring – Symbol of the Bishop's Authority – This is the signet of authority. It is worn on the right hand (the hand that represents God given authority) just as Christ sits on the right hand of God the Father. It also represents that they are committed and dedicated to Christ and His Church.

Crozier – Shepherds Staff/Tool – A symbol of the Shepherd's staff given to Moses as he was exiled from Egypt. It is the symbol of authority and strength. David declared in the Scriptures``…thy rod and they staff they comfort me…" Psalm 23

I sincerely hope that you can appreciate the purpose for vestments a little more, having increased in knowledge and understanding concerning them. With that said there is an old saying that bears repeating " It's not the clothes that make the man but the man that makes the clothes." In other words though the garments may have significance and meaning, they are only as Holy as the men that wear them. We must be mindful to *"walk worthy of the vocation wherewith we are called" Eph 4:1 Isaiah tells us to "Be ye clean, that bear the vessels of the LORD".* This is not as much about the person as it is about the principal. God established the principal and appoints the person. The person may change the principal remains the same. Therefore it is important for us to understand and embrace the principal, that in the event the person falls or fails that we don't stumble or lose faith. I know of pastors that won't wear any liturgical garments because they feel they have no significance or they think that the wearing of such garments make you self righteous, arrogant or high minded. When just the opposite is true. You see the adorning of proper liturgical garments is the ultimate sign of humility. You are laying down your own identity, you are agreeing with God. You are saying to the world and all those that see you that I am not my own, neither are the words that I speak but I represent the most High God.

We easily understand the need for uniform and rank identification in the arms forces, governmental positions and law enforcement agencies. Each color and uniform design represents a rank or position. Gods was the same, lets not presume to be wiser than God. I'm not saying that you need to wear liturgical garments or change the dress code for the leaders in your church. I'm just saying don't despise what you don't understand. I have a very healthy respect for those that make higher levels of commitment and dedicate themselves to the degree that they are willing to forfeit self expression and individuality for their love of God.

I will conclude this subject by giving this brief analogy. We that live in America are painfully aware of the fact that there are crooked police officers and other law enforcement agents in our cities and communities. However in spite of that obvious fact, we still must respect every law enforcement agent. We do not have the authority to refuse the instruction or command of a law enforcement agent based on our assumption or understanding that they may be corrupt. We are not required to respect the person, but the office in which they stand. They have superiors that they have to answer to in the event of their own mis- conduct. While we all can agree that both our legal and judicial systems are flawed, we still have if not the best, certainly one of the best systems of government in the world. Unlike our system, God's system of judg- ment is not flawed, its is perfect and it doesn't require our help or approval. *Rom 12:19 Dearly beloved, avenge not yourselves, but rather give place unto wrath: for it is written, Vengeance is mine; I will repay, saith the Lord.* Remember the old saying "One bad apple doesn't spoil the whole bunch" don't think that because a few people have perverted the purpose of the robes that the principal is lost. To the pure all things are pure. We often talk about taking back those things that the devil has stolen from us. How about we take back the sanctity of those things that God gave the church, but the enemy has perverted.

I say to those that don't think there is any significance in the robes or garments, tell that to the woman with the issue of blood who said in *Matthew 9:21 "If I may but touch his garment, I shall be whole"*. I can only speak for myself today, that when I am adorned in what is commonly known as liturgical choir dress, I feel most anointed and often wonder if this is what Aaron felt when the scrip- ture says in Psalm 133:2 that the ointment ran down Aaron's beard and went down to the skirts of his garments; It's not the garment but what and who the garment represents.

"Make holy garments for Aaron thy brother, and his sons, that he may minister unto me in the priest's office"
Exodus 28:4

Chapter 6
The Scepter

A scepter according to Webster's dictionary is defined as a wand or staff carried as the badge of command and sovereignty of kingly office or power. This is most accurately exemplified in the book of Esther 4:11 *All the king's servants, and the people of the king's provinces, do know, that whosoever, whether man or woman, shall come unto the king into the inner court, who is not called, there is one law of his to put him to death, except such to whom the king shall hold out the golden scepter, that he may live:* It is with the sovereignty of the scepter that the king may over rule the written law. The importance of the scepter was universally understood amongst the people.

To have the scepter extended towards you was to have the favor of he king extended towards you. One of the most valuable assets one can posses is favor. Favor can get you what money can't buy, what credit can't approve, it can open doors that all our educational and academic accolades cannot. Its value is immeasurable and is of absolute necessity to be successful in any kingdom or municipality. Long before David became king he found favor with the king; *1 Sam 16:21-22 And David came to Saul, and stood before him: and he loved him greatly; and he became his armor bearer. 22 And Saul sent to Jesse, saying, Let David, I pray thee, stand before me; for he hath found favor in my sight.* It's interesting how God will use favor to separate us from our peers and our brethren in order to position us for success in the kingdom. Like Abram who found favor with God, Moses who found favor with the daughter of pharaoh, and Joseph whose favor with his father eventually led to his involuntary separation and exile from his family and his people. Likewise I'm sure that David was uncertain and perhaps even insecure about his status in the family and how much more in the kingdom. As he tended the flock of his father, uninvited to the feast and overlooked as a potential candidate for royal appointment. Yet clear to the prophet that the scepter, the favor of God was upon his life. Like David, Joseph and several others including our Lord and Savior himself, our family and those who are closest to us are the last to recognize the favor of God that is upon our lives. However Ester is the exception to the rule, her cousin Mordecai saw in her beauty and favor that could certainly benefit her people.

Favor is the most valuable commodity that you have. But favor alone, that is favor without knowledge and wisdom is of limited use. Therefore as we increase in knowledge, understanding and wisdom we shall increase in favor. *Luke 2:52 And Jesus increased in wisdom and stature, and in favor with God and man.* Likewise *Proverbs 3:1-4 says My son, forget not my law; but let thine heart keep my commandments: 2 For length of days, and long life, and peace, shall they add to thee. 3 Let not mercy and truth forsake thee: bind them about thy neck; write them upon the table of thine heart: 4 So shalt thou find favor and good understanding in the sight of God and man.* Many Christians feel as though they only need the favor of God to be successful, but the bible clearly notes the need for favor with both God and man. If the Lord is going to use you in any capacity it is important that you have a good rapport with men in and outside the kingdom. Everything that God has ever done in the earth he has used a man to do it. Once creation was completed God turned over all responsibility to Adam *Gen 2:20 And Adam gave names to all cattle, and to the fowl of the air, and to every beast of the field;* From Genesis to Revelation we see God raising up men in the earth do His will in the earth. If we are going to see the favor of God manifested in our lives we must know the importance of establishing and maintaining relationships.

In chapter three I refer to covenant relationships and the importance of maintaining them. There are many things that God will do to position us for greatness and promotion. None of which can affectively materialize without the help of others, many of which may not seem to be likely candidates but God in his sovereignty and omniscience predestines all things according to his will.

Esther's example of favor coming from an unlikely source is an inspiration to all of us, let us examine: *Esther 2:15-17 Now when the turn of Esther, the daughter of Abihail the uncle of Mordecai, who had taken her for his daughter, was come to go in unto the king, she required nothing but what Hegai the king's chamberlain, the keeper of the women, appointed. And Esther obtained favor in the sight of all them that looked upon her. 16 So Esther was taken unto king Ahasuerus into his house royal in the tenth month, which is the month Tebeth, in the seventh year of his reign. 17 And the king loved Esther above all the women, and she obtained grace and favor in his sight more than all the virgins; so that he set the royal crown upon her head, and made her queen instead of Vashti.*

Initially it may seem rather carnal for ones exterior beauty to be the reason she obtained such favor, but God knows the heart of the king. There was a greater purpose involved, the future and destiny of an entire nation was at stake. As we continue to read we see that Esther possessed more that just physical beauty, she also had wisdom and grace that complimented her physical beauty. Her physical beauty was not enough, for that was the criteria for each woman to be considered for candidacy. It was her wisdom, her inner beauty that separated her from all of her peers. Though much time and consideration was given to her appearance, it was important that she possessed that intangible quality, that extra something. The development of character and integrity which is something that many talented and gifted people often lack. Our gifts and talents represent that outer beauty that may position us for favor, but it is our inner beauty, the character that is developed in us, the wisdom that is imparted to us that separates us from our peers and causes the favor of God to be extended towards us.

I said all of that to say this. I think that it is very important to give time and focus to the development of our natural gifts, abilities and talents. Whether through increasing education, our relentless pursuit of excellence in the completion projects, or the establishing and pursuit of life goals. All of which can produce success but not necessarily produce integrity, character or wisdom. In Esther's case God used Mordecai to raise her, to develop character and conviction in her, to give a sense of responsibility and commitment to her people. But the development that she would need to impress the king would come from within the kings own gates, a eunuch whose responsibility was to prepare the virgins for presentation to the king. Esther found favor and appeared to be given special treatment. *Esther 2:9And the maiden pleased him, and she obtained kindness of him; and he speedily gave her things for purification, with such things as belonged to her, and seven maidens, which were meet to be given her, out of the king's house: and he preferred her and her maids unto the best place of the house of the women.* Like Esther we all need favor to reach our destiny. Our path or process is divinely appointed, as Job said *"he knoweth the way that I take": when he hath tried me, I shall come forth as gold.* Job 23:10 No doubt orphaned and in enslaved, her future looked dark and uncertain, but those were precisely the circumstances that God needed to position her for favor.

The thing that appeared to be a disadvantage became the catalyst for her promotion. Another confirmation that all things to work together for good for those that love God and are called according to his purpose. That is why we cannot allow our past disposition or our current circumstances to frame our thinking, our purpose or our destiny.

We must rise in the face of adversity, walk in faith and trust that the Lord has purpose in our pain. As did Esther, if we are to have the king's scepter extended towards us we must find that unique balance between faith, wisdom, boldness and humility... *Esther 5:1-3 Now, it came to pass on the third day, that Esther put on her royal apparel, and stood in the inner court of the king's house, over against the king's house: and the king sat upon his royal throne in the royal house, over against the gate of the house. 2 And it was so, when the king saw Esther the queen standing in the court, that she obtained favor in his sight: and the king held out to Esther the golden scepter that was in his hand. So Esther drew near, and touched the top of the scepter. 3 Then said the king unto her, What wilt thou, queen Esther? and what is thy request? it shall be even given thee to the half of the kingdom.*

Once the scepter was extended Esther was not only accepted but protected. Like Esther you have the favor of the King, God almighty has extended His scepter towards you. His favor is upon you, you have been excepted and you are protected. Don't underestimate the favor you have, it may be that favor that God uses to "save your people.

Chapter 7

The Palace

One of the quintessential assets of any king or kingdom is a palace that provides both the luxurious comfort, as well as the impenetrable protection needed to effectively govern his providence. We are all familiar with the old saying " A man is king of his castle" while most of us if not all of us have not been blessed to live in a castle or palace, there is some truth to that statement. Unlike the humble abode that I call home, a palace represents more that just shelter, a place to lay your head or a place of comfort and relaxation. The palace was the symbol of wealth and status. Great attention was given to every detail so as to please the king and to impress his guest. It was the perfect combination of luxury and security. Quaint enough to feel like home and spacious enough to host the largest of banquets and social events. It was the pride and joy of any king to boast of having the most extravagant palace of his time. While we must be careful not to become consumed with the acquisition and accumulation of houses and material possessions, it certainly is understandable why such things are of great significance to those of royal descent. In ancient days such things helped define a king's life and legacy. Which is why when a king would conquer another king and his territory, he would completely destroy it. He would level the city and anything that reminded people of the glory of the former king.

Thus establishing himself as the supreme ruler and ultimate authority in the land. Which in part explains why Jesus teaches us to pray " let thy kingdom come" because for His kingdom to come, ours must go, it must be destroyed, obliterated completely demolished. We surrender power and control to Him, He becomes King and we are His subjects. Unlike a conquering king who enslaves his subjects and forces his will upon them, our king insist on being invited to power. He has neither need nor desire for forced servitude or insincere worship and praise. He is most noted as the "King of kings" and yet the mere conquering of earthly kingdoms can neither add too, nor take away from His infinite wisdom, power and glory.

The model of a kingdom and attributes of a king are demonstrated and illustrated strictly for our benefit. God is not some narcissistic ego maniac that needs the solicited praise of mankind to validate his majesty. It is when we come into the knowledge of His kingdom that He reveals to us the essence of His glory. Once enlightened we are compelled from within to serve in His kingdom, to worship at His feet and to lead others in the path of righteousness. Many people outside of the kingdom don't understand why we put so much focus on excellence, an in some opinions extravagance in the house of God. It is because He is our king and the church is His palace, so we prioritize the house of God without apology. We spare no expense because the palace represents the Glory of its King. The closer we get to God the more we understand His kingdom, and the next logical response is to provide a palace fit for His dwelling.

The Palace is more for us than for Him. He is omnipresent, He is in all places at the same time, and He cannot be contained within a building, by brick and mortar, but desires to dwell within the hearts of men. *"Behold, the tabernacle of God is with men, and he will dwell with them, and they shall be his people, and God himself shall be with them, and be their God."* Rev 21:3 Physical buildings have no significance if He does not live within our hearts. In the scripture whenever a house was built for God, it was because of what was in the hearts of the people. In 2 Sam 7:2 & 3 David speaks to Nathan and says, *"See now, I dwell in an house of cedar, but the ark of God dwelleth within curtains. And Nathan said to the king, Go, do all that is in thine heart; for the LORD is with thee".* We should only put our hearts into the building when the building comes out of our hearts. *Behold, I stand at the door, and knock: if any man hear my voice, and open the door, I will come in to him, and will sup with him, and he with me. Rev 3:20* We must be careful not to focus more on opening the doors of the church than we do on opening the doors of our hearts. One of the most basic needs of man is to have a comfortable, secure place to live. I think the same can be said of man's spirit to have a comfortable, secure place to worship. While the need for a suitable structure is paramount, there should be equal importance placed on its ambiance and environment. Those things that make a house a home. The things that money cannot buy, what décor and design cannot produce. The spirit of the house. I don't want a house, a church, an office not even an automobile that God won't dwell in. I'd rather live in a shack and have his presence than live in a palace without it. Like the psalmist *"I had rather be a doorkeeper in the house of my God, than to dwell in the tents of wickedness". Psalms 84:10* So while we strive to produce excellence in our churches and worship facilities, let us not for get the purpose for the structure. Its beauty is only as attractive as the spirit in those that worship within. Don't be defined by the material possessions that you amass. Don't let your legacy be limited to corruptible temporal things, but rather seek to keep your spirit pure. So that all that proceeds out of your heart will be pure and acceptable unto God. It is when we've reached this purity in spirit that the palace has transcended its earthly purpose and becomes a spiritual habitation for the lord.

1 Chronicles 29:1 "For the palace is not for man, but for the LORD God". The irony is we like David out of our sincere desire to worship and honor the lord, can build for him, that which he neither needs nor requires. But rather desires and receives solely for our benefit. The equivalent of a Father receiving with joy the macaroni necklace made by his kindergarten child who's only desire is to please his father. What an amazing God we serve.

The Palace is symbolic of many things, most importantly it represents the place where the people of God gather to worship, fellowship and hear the word of God. While we will remember its primary purpose, we also understand that in a day of multipurpose

facilities and entrepreneurial encouragement, community development, social activism and economic empowerment. The church has
had to adapt to a more multi functional role in the community. There
are so many reasons that a person might join a church today. Unfortunately these days the last reason could be the leading of the spirit of
God, or finding their shepherd or God ordained leader. After all in
our society there are so many other things to consider. Does your
church have children's ministry, day care, are you on television, how
about something for teenagers, can I come casual? How long are
your services? Do you have a choir? What about dance or drama?
Here's a good one "is there a place for me in leadership?" Those
things are just to name a few. While all of those things have a place
in our list of concerns and desires they should not top our list of pri-
orities.

While striving to meet all of the needs of the people, let us
not forget the purpose of the palace. Whether the palace seats thou-
sands, hundreds or tens, whether it is multi purpose or of single use.
Whether it is a beacon of hope or a pillar of strength, whether its
attendees are the upper echelons of society or the most common and
ordinary of people. We must strive to produce a palace worthy to be
called the "House of the Lord" and that means producing excellence!
But excellence must be defined before it can be achieved. We must
understand the difference between excellence and perfection. Perfection means to be without flaw, blemish free, and most times we find
it impossible to produce flawless or blemish free anything! Because
we are flawed and blemished, how can we, imperfect and flawed
beings produce perfection? The scripture says that "we have this treasure in earthen vessels, that the excellency of the power may be of
God, and not of us." 2 Corinthians 4:7

God knows our flaws and our imperfections, and the perfection that he requires from us would be better termed or defined as
excellence. For excellence is much different than perfection. I've
seen so many people, myself included frustrated because they were
so called "perfectionist" everything had to be perfect. Not considering the notion of calling oneself a perfectionist is an oxymoron in

that perfection can not come from imperfection. It is with that knowledge that we understand that the treasure, the perfect spirit of God is in an earthen vessel. The flawed, imperfect flesh of man. But when the spirit of man submits to the spirit of God, we can produce excellence, and the excellency is of God and not of us. That said and understood let us briefly define excellence as it pertains to the house of God.

None of us should consider ourselves perfectionist but rather people of excellence. Daniel had an excellent spirit, and it was that spirit that caused him to prosper. ***A person with a spirit of excellence will always do the best they can with what they have.*** That person will always strive to do better because perfection is now unattainable by its current definition. But excellence can be achieved through the planning, maximizing and execution of a God given vision. And now we have come full circle *"For the palace is not for man, but for the LORD God"*. So we serve the Lord with a perfect heart and with an excellent spirit and His majesty the King graciously receives our offering. "What a mighty God we serve"

Chapter 8

Connected to the wrong King

You're connected to a king who has all of the attributes of a king. A throne, a palace a scepter, a crown and all the other things that make a king legitimate. But what if all those things are superseded by the fact that either the anointing or your grace to submit to this king is gone. This is a very important subject that must be addressed in the Body of Christ. Where should your loyalty be when God has rejected your leader? What causes God to reject a leader? Is it disobedience? Is it rebellion? Is it weakness, sin, arrogance, pride or simply that ones time is up? Just as I stated in the introduction, when God sets up a leader it is a sovereign act. He doesn't consult with us, nor does he care about our leadership criteria. The same holds true when He removes, rejects or retires a leader.

Leading up to our principle story, the kingdom of Israel has had only one king, that being king Saul who ultimately was rejected by God. *1 Sam 13:13-14 And Samuel said to Saul, Thou hast done foolishly: thou hast not kept the commandment of the LORD thy God, which he commanded thee: for now would the LORD have established thy kingdom upon Israel for ever. But now thy kingdom shall not continue: the LORD hath sought him a man after his own heart, and the LORD hath commanded him to be captain over his people, because thou hast not kept that which the LORD commanded thee.* It was always God's desire to be Israel's King. "*But the thing displeased Samuel, when they said, Give us a king to judge us. And Samuel prayed unto the LORD. And the LORD said unto Samuel, Hearken unto the voice of the people in all that they say unto thee: for they have not rejected thee, but they have rejected me, that I should not reign over them." 1 Sam 8:6-7* When Israel rejected the Lord as king, He in turn gave them a king after their own heart. His disobedience, self will and pride would eventually and inevitably be exposed and uncovered, as is the case with all leaders as Jesus clearly declares and explains in *John 10:13 The hireling fleeth, because he is an hireling, and careth not for the sheep.* Saul's primary concern was himself and not the people of Israel. While some may beg to differ, I submit to you that many have done good deeds, noble works and dare I say heroic exploits with impure motives. Whether driven by ambition, motivated by greed or inspired by the power of position and authority. Good leadership skills are not enough to warrant undying loyalty and unquestioned submission as some would suggest and even require in many cases. As I mentioned in chapter two, a Godly connection is very unique and is often times accompanied by an unexplainable commitment and loyalty to the person and not the position. Which is how the enemy is successful in exploiting and misleading the saints. The principle of delegated authority and submission to leaders has been taught to an almost unhealthy degree.

We merely have to look to Saul and those connected to him as our example. Once it was apparent that God had rejected Saul and chosen David to be king, (which by the way was a single act in expression but not in execution). Saul remained in power many years after the Lord had rejected him king, which makes this subject of very sensitive and delicate nature. I want to be very careful not to send the wrong message, because the scripture implies that Saul, his son Jonathan as well as many of the men that were with him heard the prophet as he declared the Lord's judgment concerning Saul.

Where should your loyalty be when God has rejected your leader?

It is clear that rejection and removal are two entirely different things and it is important that we discern the difference. There are a number of reasons why we cannot move ahead of God and His plan concerning our fallen leaders. The first being that God is a merciful God and gives us opportunity and space to repent. During that time it is our responsibility to pray for our leader and not to pass judgment or seek to undermine their authority. It always amazes me how little grace we have for our leaders. Whether spiritual, political, corporate or secular. While leaders should be held to a higher standard, *"my brethren, be not many masters, knowing that we shall receive the greater condemnation." James 3:1* We must be careful not to pass judgment prematurely or too severely. *Matt 7:2 For with what judgment ye judge, ye shall be judged: and with what measure ye mete, it shall be measured to you again.* God has his own timing, and most times His timing is not our timing. One of the worst things we can do is leave too soon or stay too long.

There are some things that can only be discerned by the spirit of the Lord, but that discernment can be aided by some practical observations that can help us to make wise decisions. I certainly do not claim to be an expert on the subject therefore I will not seek to explain or examine every circumstance, but will look at just a few of what I consider major situations in which you should separate from a leader. The first is that you have a sure word from God. If you know the voice of God and you are certain or at least believe with all your heart that you have heard God say that you need to disconnect from your leader, then you must obey God. God in His infinite wisdom knows what is best for us and our leader. It is important to note that in this circumstance we are reminded that we are unaware as to the Lord's reasons or intentions in disconnecting us from our leader. It would be irresponsible and presumptuous for us to assume that God has rejected the leader. It may simply be that our time is up or our purpose has been fulfilled with that leader.

I can use a personal example of such an instance. In 2000 one of my most faithful members and true sons of my ministry came to me and said that he had an opportunity for both ministry and vocation that would require him to relocate and leave the ministry. At the time I didn't want to lose him and his family but I also didn't want to hold him back. So I released him and his family with my blessing. That was over eight years ago and in that time the Lord has more than provided for the needs of my ministry as well has taken him all over the nation, opening tremendous doors. The whole time using the word and lessons that I had placed in him.

Long story short, though he separated, he never disconnected and now the Lord has planted him and raised him up in ministry. I had the privilege of installing him as Pastor just recently and I could not have been more proud. But none of that could happen without us separating in Gods time. It's not always negative, many times the Lord is just preparing you for your next level. I'll never forget some of the many phone conversations he and I had and the many times he has said to me "I'm so glad that when I left, I left right" and I would reply "I'm so glad I let you leave right" I've heard pastors say for years that if you are going to leave, just make sure you leave right. And I've watched some of those same pastors make it impossible for anyone to leave right. But when God says go we may not understand it but we must separate and try not to disconnect. Do all that is within your ability to leave right and maintain relationship. If that is not possible then leave quietly without incident and trust the Lord to do the rest.

There are times when you feel you need to separate from a leader and you don't have a clear word from God. What do you do then? What are some circumstances in which that is acceptable? Well, let's start with the most obvious of situations, and that is when a leader clearly is no longer committed to the standards of Godly and biblical leadership that drew you to them initially. That is to say their lifestyle is not becoming of a Godly leader. Meaning that there has been more that just a moral failure but a clear abandonment of morality with no desire to repent. We are not speaking of liberties exercised or even abused but laws blatantly broken with no regard to consequence or responsibility.

In such cases when you can no longer submit to a leader in good conscience, you should leave in the same manor previously described. Quietly and discretely so as not to disrupt ministry or offend others who may not feel the same way that you do. In this circumstance your responsibility is to your own spiritual well being and not to expose or contaminate others who may be growing and receiving from that ministry. It is not your responsibility to judge or expose that leader, for they are not your anointed but Gods, and He said, *"Touch not mine anointed, and do my prophets no harm."* *1st Chronicles 16:22* God has his own way of dealing with His leaders and it is our best interest to leave that to Him.

The third and final scenario that I want to look at, is when it has been determined that a leader is, as the scripture says, a wolf, a hireling or a heretic. That is to say, not a Godly leader at all. What do your do in such cases, do you just leave, separate, disconnect or do you have a greater responsibility? Should you warn others and if so who? Were do you start? Let me start by reiterating that I would not and do not recommend having a pastor that does not have a pastor. We all need accountability for our own protection as well as for the protection of those that are committed to our care. That accountability may come through a spiritual father or mentor, a governing board, or even a group of credible peers. There must be some authoritative figure who can confront us with correction , reproof or rebuke if necessary. The absence of such an authority is recipe for disaster even for the most sincere and committed leader. There must be safe guards to protect us from the traps and temptations of the enemy as well as the frailty of our own flesh.

When properly established the course of action is clear, you must first confront the leader and if necessary the leaders leader. Not with rumors or conjecture but with sincere concern about behavior or improper practices that have been confirmed and are undeniable, considering the scriptures instructions. *"Against an elder receive not an accusation, but before two or three witnesses."* *1 Tim 5:19* With that said we must not entertain rumors and unfounded allegations and we certainly should not rely on premonitions or gut feelings. These cases are rare and should be handled with the utmost care and discretion. Once you have followed the proper protocol your job is done. As long as the leaders actions are not illegal or a danger, threat or in any way harmful to others, that is to say a danger to those that cannot protect themselves, such as children ect. And even in extreme cases you should attempt to leave in the same manor described in the previous two scenarios.

In any case when you are sure that you are connected to the wrong leader you should separate and move on to the next phase of your life. I often read books or watch movies in search of quips, quotes and anecdotes that help express or illuminate a point. One of the most profound concerning separation is from the movie "The War of the Roses" Danny De Vito's character makes the statement **"The two hardest things to do are to make someone go that wants to stay, and to make someone stay that wants to go"** How true that is, many times we either stay too long or leave too soon. When it came to Saul and David, Jonathon new that David was God's man. In his effort not to leave too soon he stayed too long and he died a premature death. We cannot allow our natural or carnal relationships to dictate or control our spiritual destinies. Jesus said *"a man's foes shall be they of his own household. He that loveth father or mother more than me is not worthy of me: Matt 10:36-37* We cannot seek to know one another after the flesh. Our allegiance must be first to the Lord Jesus Christ and then to those that he has positioned in our lives to lead us in the path of righteousness. Don't die following Saul when God has already revealed the David in your life. God will deal with both Saul and David in His own time, make sure you are connected to the right king.

"The two hardest things to do are to make someone go that wants to stay, and to make someone stay that wants to go"

Chapter 9

In between kingdoms

At this point in David's life he has come through many struggles following his anointing by Samuel the prophet. As with many of us (if not all of us) it is a long journey from "anointing to appointing" So was the case with David, he has been called from the back fields tending his fathers sheep. He has killed the lion and the bear, he has even slain the mighty giant, the enemy of Israel, Goliath. He has survived King Saul's threatening, endured the brutal caves of Abdullah and avenged the savage invasion of Ziklag. Saul and Jonathan are now dead. The end of an era, the reign of Israel's first king has come to a tragic end. In 1st Samuel 31 we have the details of the deaths of Saul, his sons and all of his men. Verse six in particular stands out to me *"So Saul died, and his three sons, and his armour bearer, and all his men, that same day together."* Saul's kingdom had a purpose and when that purpose had been fulfilled, it and all those connected to it was brought to an end. But woe be unto those that seek promotion through the downfall of another, those opportunist. It is the Lord who sets up one and brings down another. The most notable thing about 1st Samuel chapter thirty one is that David's name is not so much as mentioned in it. When God rejects a leader He and He alone knows how to bring them down and when He does, it would behoove us not to have our names mentioned in that chapter. Let it not be said of us that like the Amalekite who thought himself to be the bearer of good news to David concerning Saul and his sons. That we are not afraid to stretch forth our hands towards God's anointed. For in doing so we jeopardize our own future and destiny. *"And David said unto him, Thy blood be upon thy head; for thy mouth hath testified against thee, saying, I have slain the Lord's anointed."* 2 Sam 1:16 David appropriately laments the deaths of Saul and Jonathan and then he inquires of the Lord " shall I go up?" He takes nothing for granted, he must hear from God. We cannot assume that it is our time based solely on the opportunity that is before us. The Lord answers David and instructs him to go up to Hebron and it was there that David was anointed king over Judah. In the mean time Ishbosheth, Saul's son is reigning as King over Israel. But all is not well in the kingdom.

There is much uncertainty about Israel's future but the unification of the kingdom seems to be inevitable. There is war between the house of David and the house of Saul, but the scripture says that the house of David waxed stronger and stronger and the house of Saul waxed weaker and weaker. In 2nd Samuel chapter three we see the final stages of the translation of the kingdom unfolding. It's an incredible story and I definitely recommend reading it in its entirety, (1 Sam 16 through 2 Sam 4) from anointing to appointing. I will however, for the sake our story and the development of our point provide a brief synopsis of the drama unfolding at this point in David's life. David is in very unfamiliar territory. In many ways at the pinnacle of success and in others at the beginning of trials. Or as the saying goes "with new levels, come new devils" We must prepare for the problems that accompany promotion. We must exercise wisdom and patience, as James said, let patience have its perfect work that you may be entire wanting nothing.

The kingdom is now in a very unstable state. Israel, haven gotten its much desired king, they were now like other nations around them facing some of the same problems and these for the first time. The transfer of the kingdom, the rejected king is dead and according to custom and tradition the throne should be ascended by the heir, the son of the king. But God not only rejected king Saul himself but his entire family and even his tribe Benjamin from being king. God had chosen the tribe of Judah, but the tribe of Judah suffered a great setback as a result of Judah's illegitimate children Pharez and Zarah by

Tamar his daughter in law. According to the law in *Deut 23:2 A bas-tard shall not enter into the congregation of the LORD; even to his tenth generation shall he not enter into the congregation of the LORD.*

Sin will always delay our divine appointment, but we find that even in our sinful state, God in His omniscience predestines us according to His own purpose. So for ten generations God was preparing His King, *Matt 1:3-6 Judas begat Phares and Zara of Thamar; and Phares begat Esrom; and Esrom begat Aram; And Aram begat Aminadab; and Aminadab begat Naasson; and Naasson begat Salmon; And Salmon begat Booz of Rachab; and Booz begat Obed of Ruth; and Obed begat Jesse;* ***And Jesse begat David the king.*** No wonder David said in *Ps 122:1 "I was glad when they said unto me, Let us go into the house of the LORD".* With all the prophetic words and divine interventions, David is still unfulfilled. Pleased I'm sure to be king of Judah but undoubtedly wondering if the full promise will ever come to pass. Many of God's chosen have endured long, tedious periods of trial and testing before experiencing a glimpse of the promise, but a true visionary will hold fast to that promise. *"Though the vision tarry, wait for it" Habbakah 2:3* David has exercised great patience up until this point and once again there is no reason to become irrational or unstable. So David wisely is content to reign in Hebron until God elevates him, while Ishbosheth's paranoia and other insecurities are starting to loosen his already weakened grip on the kingdom.

At this point Ishbosheth's strongest supporter and ally is Abner the captain of Saul's army. Abner is a fierce warrior with stature, respect and political savvy as well. Ishbosheth is inexperienced and lacks diplomacy and unwisely accuses Abner of lying with his fathers concubine, not only is this a very serious accusation as well as a pretty blatant insult, it also brings into question Abner's loyalty. Abner is now forced to make a decision, continue to support an inexperienced, incompetent and now equally insulting puppet king, or join David, God's choice. While the decision seems to be quote "a no brainer" there are many other variables to consider. Abner can defect to David with little or no consequence from Ishbosheth, but in doing so he will be forced to deal with his most recent past. Nevertheless he sent messengers to David and set a meeting.

In II Samuel chapter two we find Abner and Joab sportingly sparing against one another at the expense of the young men under their command. The Bible say's that there was a fierce battle that day and that Abner was beaten and began to retreat. His retreat would be slightly hindered by the pursuit of Asahel, Joab's younger brother. Upon recognizing young Asahel, Abner begins to plead with him to turn back and give up his pursuit. Live to fight another day as it were, but there was no persuading this young, talented but perhaps over zealous warrior. Perhaps this is why the scripture says that wisdom is better than weapons of war, for the lack of wisdom would cost the young warrior his life. Abner was left with no choice, it was either kill, or be killed. Any sane, rational person would choose the latter. So it was, in an instance, Abner had taken his spear and thrust it into Asahel, and Asahel died that day. Joab unaware or perhaps unconcerned about Abner's explicit and fare warnings pursued Abner until he finally came to his senses, heard the words of Abner and blew a trumpet calling off this bloody battle. Though the battle may have subsided, the rage in Joab's heart over the slaying of his brother would never die.

David on the other hand, undoubtedly excited about the coming news of Abner's alliance with him, is eagerly anticipating the end of war and the reuniting of the kingdom under his rule. David and Abner's meeting has ended with the success anticipated by both parties and now all that is left is to celebrate the fulfillment of all that has been spoken by the prophets. While David and Abner have reached an acceptable agreement, Joab has neither been consulted nor consoled. When Joab finally returned and hears of what has happened he is furious with David, and his anger against Abner has been rekindled. The scripture says that we should guard our hearts with all diligence for out of it proceeds the issues of life. We must be careful not to allow anger and bitterness to fester in our hearts, for the end of such passions are destructive and dangerous. Joab and his brother are intent on avenging their brother's death. They give neither thought nor care to what affect it will have on the king or the kingdom. It is this attitude that is most dangerous to the king and his kingdom. Those that would put their own desires and ambitions above the desires of the king are the kingdoms greatest threat. The enemy is expected to do everything within his power to hinder, delay and even deny our ascension to our God given prophetic purpose and destiny, but many times it is not the enemy that causes our delay but those who are closest to us. Those that we trust and depend on.

Walking close to a leader should always be viewed as a privilege and an honor, not a right or an entitlement. We must always remind ourselves that our duty is to serve the king and the interest of the kingdom, and never to allow our own ambitions to distract us. As with the natural body, if any body part were to rebel against the head or the rest of the body we would not hesitate to do what ever is necessary to bring order to the body. Even if it would call for the amputation of that limb or body part. The survival of the whole is far more important than the retention of any one part.

The decisions that we make while in subordinate positions are the ones that not only shape our character but also reveal our thoughts, motives and intents. It's been said and I've found it to be true. Success and promotion doesn't change who we are, it reveals who we are. If you want to know what kind of leader you will be, look at what kind of follower you have been. David was an exemplary follower, in times of discomfort and uncertainty he remained steadfast, loyal and faithful. Even when others felt he was well within his rights to aggressively pursue the throne, David was content to wait on the Lord. He is a great example of how to behave when in between kingdoms or assignments. Joab on the other hand reveals to us the dangers of allowing our personal feelings and opinions to override our commitment to our call and purpose. We should all learn from Joab's mistakes and endeavor to put the interest of the king and kingdom ahead of our own. Joab's unrestrained anger and bitterness toward Abner would ultimately cloud his judgment and cause him to disregard the wishes of the king. Joab would quickly render Abner and David's alliance ineffective by assassinating the would be defector. The description of Abner's death, has a lesson in it as well. In fact David's lamentation also gives a cautionary warning to all of us. *2 Sam 3:33-34 And the king lamented over Abner, and said, Died Abner as a fool dieth? Thy hands were not bound, nor thy feet put into fetters: as a man falleth before wicked men, so fellest thou. And all the people wept again over him.* David implies that Abnor has some responsibility in his own death, in that he should have known better. He should have never put himself in such a vulnerable position. An unwise decision can cost you a fortune, but a foolish one can cost you your life. Abner's decision wasn't just unwise it was foolish. The Bible says in *Proverbs 27:6 "Faithful are the wounds of a friend; but the kisses of an enemy are deceitful."* While there are several lessons in this short verse the most important is to know who your friends are as well as your enemies.

Joab had never been a friend to Abner and it was foolish of Abner to think that a single act or gesture would change that. If anything Abner's alliance with David would pose a threat to Joab. As leaders we are always praying for more help, and it becomes very frustrating when God sends competent and qualified help and you find you can't use them because of the jealousy and insecurity of your current staff. David is once again delayed, the vision must tarry yet another season, though short, another set back none the less. The lesson learned is that while in between kingdoms we must continue to be steadfast and unwavering, even when the obstacles blocking us are not of our own doing.

"If you want to know what kind of leader you will be, look at what kind of follower you have been."

Chapter 10

Weak though Anointed

2nd Sam 3:39 ***I am this day weak, though anointed king;***
David now finds himself in a position that many leaders can identify
with. We've finally made it, all the years of struggle and holding on,
believing in God and yourself have seemingly paid off. Seventeen
years from anointing to appointing, a journey that should cause us all
to reflect upon and consider our own paths. Undoubtedly your story
is unique, inspiring and perhaps even heroic. No matter how dramatic
or moving, I am certain that none of our stories could compare to that
of King David's. Yet amazingly through every trial and set back,
David manages to maintain his poise and keep his cool. He has survived every scuffle with the enemies of his fathers flock, the lion and
the bear, he has fearlessly slain the mighty Goliath who dared to defy
the armies of the Living God. As captain of Saul's army he has countless victories over the Philistines, he has survived Saul's threatening
and attacks. He has even avenged the cowardly attack on Ziklag,
when at one of his lowest points, a time when he was greatly dis-
tressed because the people spake of stoning him, David is able to
encourage himself in the Lord. David has shown nothing but courage
and strength throughout his life, so what is it about this moment that
changes his confession what is it that causes him to declare his weakness in the presence of the people?

Many of us, like David have been taught and trained not to
show weakness, "never let them see you sweat." However I believe
David has finally come the realization that no matter how much he

has it together, no matter how "on the ball he is" no matter how many good decisions he makes or great plans and visions he has, no matter how great his anointing is, his plans can be rendered ineffective and his kingdom thereby weakened by the actions of another.

Wow! What a blow this must have been for David, realizing that he could have done everything right, dotted every I and crossed every T and still have been delayed and possibly even denied, all because of the uncontrolled anger of another. But this is not just any other person, this is Joab, David's right hand man, an extension of himself. A man appointed by David. Therefore, even when acting without the consent of the king, he is operating in the authority of the king. I have often said that the only person that can stop me from reaching my God ordained destiny is me. And like David, I have come to the realization that though that statement may be correct, it is also incomplete. There is simply more to it than that. Any person that has ever been in a position of authority knows that their subordinates are an extension of themselves and in many cases represent you. If they make good decisions we receive the credit, and likewise if they make poor decisions we receive the blame. So as a leader you are faced with some difficult choices, you can either be controlling , overbearing and micro manage everything so as to limit anyone else's authority or input, or you can undertake the daunting task of training and developing and even trusting your leaders. The dichotomy is that if you seek to fully insolate yourself, you will ultimately isolate and limit yourself.

Where there is no risk, there is no reward and the same holds true with the measures of little and much. You will never be a successful leader without having vulnerabilities, it is inevitable, but you can calculate and manage your risk and vulnerabilities so as to maximize success and minimize failures. But make no mistake about it, you will have some failures, it is impossible to succeed without them. Ultimately Joab and leaders like him will pay for there own sins. When David heard what happened he said, *"I and my kingdom are guiltless before the LORD for ever from the blood of Abner the son of Ner: Let it rest on the head of Joab, and on all his father's house;*

and let there not fail from the house of Joab one that hath an issue, or that is a leper, or that leaneth on a staff, or that falleth on the sword, or that lacketh bread." Joab was reprimanded but not removed, and this would not be the last time Joab would cause the king great anxiety, perhaps we should learn from David's mistake.

Once it is determined that a person cannot perform their duties dispassionately. That is to say without involving their personal feelings or opinions, no matter how gifted or talented that person may be, it may be in our best interest to remove that person or at least limit their influence before their uncontrolled anger or ambition costs us much more than we are willing to pay. David lost an ally at the hands of Joab and he would eventually lose a son. How many good people have you lost because of leaders that lack either the people skills they need to retain people or they are constantly sabotaging your recruiting efforts. People are drawn to and joined to a leader, but many times it is those that will interact with them most that determines their commitment level, which brings us to this point.

The most valuable and critical asset of any king, president, pastor, bishop, leader or manager of any kind is the people he or she has around them. The subordinate leaders, those that are extensions of the leader, those that require your trust and faith and support. All other components of ministry and business are easily manageable and even fixable in a relative sense. If you have facility problems that's an easy fix, that is to say the solution can be narrowed down to executable options. Whether to move to a new facility. Rent, lease, purchase, downsize, expand or even consolidate. It simply comes down to a matter of properly calculating the most efficient move and executing that move with precision. Sure there are other variables that come into play, but all things being equal, if all of our success was dependent upon our ability to make the right decision and execute, we would have significantly fewer setbacks. Because we are dependant upon the actions of others, we are connected to one anothers successes and failures, and to a great degree our futures and destinies are intertwined. Therefore it would behoove us to know those that labor among us and certainly lay hands upon no man suddenly but prove all things. Understanding that we cannot eliminate risk and vulnerabilities but we can minimize them by using wisdom and exercising a little caution when appointing leaders. That being said, if we are to be successful, than we must trust those that serve with us. For in them lies our true strength or as the old saying goes "a chain is only as strong as its weakest link" When you except an appointed position, you must receive it as the taking of an oath or a vow. Your loyalty must be unquestioned and your commitment unchallenged. We must be ever reminded of our purpose, and that purpose is to help bring to pass the vision of our leader. You must understand that you are the strength of your leader, like Aaron and Hur *in Exodus 17:11-12 when Moses held up his hand Israel prevailed: and when he let down his hand, Amalek prevailed. But Moses' hands were heavy; and **they** took a stone, and put it under him, and he sat thereon; and Aaron and Hur stayed up his hands, the one on the one side, and the other on the other side; and his hands were steady until the going down of the sun.* When Moses was weak Israel would lose the battle. The battle was not won through Moses' strength alone. As inevitable as it was with Moses, our strength is limited and will deplete before long. The only hope we have of winning the battles that we face is that we are surrounded by competent, trustworthy people who will put the wellbeing of the their leader and people above their own. Joshua and his army had a battle plan I'm sure, but his best laid plans were not enough. When his strength was exhausted he needed the strength of his leader, but what happens when your leader is weak, when his strength has decayed, what do you do then? There must be someone in position to under gird that leader. To lend him their strength, to place a stone under him, that is to say a solid foundation, to hold up his hands, the hands always represent strength. To provide strength to strength.

Individually our strength is very limited, but collectively our strength is immeasurable. The Bible says in *Deut 32:30 that one should chase a thousand, and two put ten thousand to flight.* When we come together our strength is not simply added together but it is multiplied. If that is true when we come together and support our leader, then its converse would be true as well. David should have had his strength multiplied, but because of the selfish acts of Joab he instead would have his strength weakened. Addition always equals multiplication in the kingdom, division always equals subtraction. How many times has the kingdom been weakened by our selfish actions and ambitions? How many setbacks has your leader suffered because addition was expected but division was experienced.

While all the other attributes and components of a kingdom are important and have significance, there is none more important than you, that's right, you are the strength of the king. You as well as those that would serve with you. You have significance, importance and relevance, don't ever forget it, and don't ever feel like you don't count, you matter, and you make a difference. You can't afford to have a bad day or an unfruitful season. You can't afford to get in a rut, the kingdom can't afford it. Your rut may spell the kings ruin. Your attitude may determine the king's altitude. Your inspiration might affect the king's expiration! Certainly we take all of that with a grain of salt, as we don't want to think more highly of ourselves than we aught to think, "don't have an exaggerated opinion of our own impor-tance" but think soberly. That said, we must properly esteem our-selves and our leaders so that together we can fulfill the will of God for our lives.

Establishing the kingdom of God in the earth should be the primary goal of every ministry in the world. We will never see the kingdom of God fully manifested if we don't understand kingdom authority and protocol. We must all surrender our will to the will of the King. That is not to say, to the Lord only, but also to the God ordained leaders that he has placed in our lives. We must completely submit to and honor the delegated authority that is placed in our lives. The kingdoms only enemies should be the devil and the world, as in *James 4:4 "know ye not that the friendship of the world is enmity with God? whosoever therefore will be a friend of the world is the enemy of God".* You are not my enemy and I hope that you don't see me as yours, no matter what our differences are, if Jesus Christ is our Lord and Savior than we are on the same team.

The Conclusion

Iron Sharpens Iron

Proverbs 27:17 Iron sharpeneth iron; so a man sharpeneth the countenance of his friend. **"Show me your friends and I'll show you your future"** no truer phrase has ever been coined. We need to surround ourselves with people that make us stronger, sharper, smarter and even wiser. *Proverbs 13:20 He that walketh with wise men shall be wise: but a companion of fools shall be destroyed.* The enemy is cunning and clever, he doesn't need you to backslide and leave God to destroy you, and he doesn't need to you to go clubbing or fall into sexual sin. He doesn't even need you to smoke, get high or take a drink. He only needs to put a fool in your life! I challenge you to look around you, and evaluate the people that are closest to you, are they strong? Strong like iron? Because if they are, they can sharpen you but if they are weak they may ultimately weaken you. One thing is for certain, either they will become more like you, or you will become more like them. If you want to be great, surround yourself with greatness, if you want to be wealthy, surround yourself with wealth. If you want to be happy, surround yourself with happy people. If you want to be healthy, well you get the point. How do you determine what type of people you are connected to? First we must define a wise man and a fool.

A fool is defined as being; stupid, vile, silly or wicked.

A wise man is intelligent, skillful, artful, cunning and subtle.

Here are a few scriptures to help us categorize the people closest to us.

*Prov 12:15 The way of a fool is **right in his own eyes**: but he that hearkeneth unto counsel is wise*

*Prov 10:23 **It is as sport** to a fool to do mischief: but a man of understanding hath wisdom.*

*Prov 11:29 He that **troubleth his own house** shall inherit the wind: and the fool shall be servant to the wise of heart.*

*Prov 10:8 The wise in heart will **receive commandments**: but a prating fool shall fall.*

*Prov 14:16 A wise man **feareth, and departeth from evil**: but the fool **rageth, and is confident.***

*Prov 28:26 He that **trusteth in his own heart** is a fool: but whoso walketh wisely, he shall be delivered.*

*Prov 29:11 A fool **uttereth all his mind:** but a wise man keepeth it in till afterwards.*

*Prov 17:10 A **reproof entereth** more into a wise man than an hundred stripes into a fool.*

The Bible is constantly warning us about the dangers of foolish companions, many of us have suffered severe consequences for not heeding those warnings. I realize that it may be impossible to cut all foolish people from our lives completely but you can keep them at a distance, only allow them limited access to you and certainly don't give them authority to act on your behalf and never under any circumstances submit yourself to a fool. That said, what about the wise man? What about that iron that sharpens iron. We must understand this concept in order to put this scripture into context. The concept is simple,

"Iron when properly used, sharpens Iron"

This can only happen when;

There is contact not connection. Many people want to be sharpened without contact and then others think that all contact must result in connection. And neither could be further from the truth. There are leaders today that can no longer be touched and therefore can no longer be sharpened because sharpening requires contact. And then some cannot be sharpened because they will only allow contact from those that want to connect, thus limiting their potential growth and development.

There is compatibility. We may not be exactly alike, in fact we appear to be opposites, but that doesn't mean that we are not compatible. Many times we cannot be sharpened because we only have contact with those who are just like us, we only see our differences and not our areas of common ground. This is a trick of the enemy to keep the Kingdom of God weak by keeping us divided based on our differences instead of us uniting based on our commonalities. Every detail doesn't have to be common, but we can be compatible if we see and embrace the big picture.

There is conflict. Iron sharpens iron by making contact on compatible areas going in conflicting directions and that produces the desired result. We must be willing to deal with confrontation and conflict if we are to be sharpened, "endure hardness" conflict is a part of life and we cannot allow every conflict to result in disconnection. We need conflict in our lives and ministries, everyone should not have the same view or opinion all of the time. If we can disagree with out disrespecting one another we can sharpen and strengthen one another.

The implication is that through this same process a man sharpens the countenance of his friend. The word friend in this text simply means companion, it could be a close friend, spouse, family member, co-worker or casual acquaintance. That suggests that we can be sharpened by almost anyone! I am always intrigued by the use of the body and body parts in the scripture to describe or explain a spiritual truth. Each body part has its own physical function as well as a metaphorical application. The hands for instance always represent strength, the eyes, perception and vision, the ears understanding but what of the face? The countenance, what does it mean to sharpen a man's countenance? What, if any significance can this have? Let us look at what the face represents.

The face expresses Image. The word image is used in the scripture figuratively to denote resemblance, likeness or a representative figure. According to *Gen 1:27 God created man in his own image, Gen 5:3 Adam begat a son in his own likeness, after his image; and called his name Seth:* In addition image is defined as the imagery produced when you are seen or thought of. There is a saying "Image is everything" that is to say, what comes to mind when others see or think of you is of great importance. When your name is mentioned in your absence there is an image that comes to mind. That image can be one of success or failure, it can produce joy or sadness, it can inspire or incapacitate. Much of the image we portray is in some way shaped or at least influenced by the people that are closest to us. Sharp people sharpen those around them. If you want an image of success, hang around successful people. Choose your friends wisely and the will sharpen your image.

The face expresses Identity. We are most easily identified by our face. You can't have a picture ID with a photo of your hand, foot or some other body part, what makes it a photo ID is that your face is on it. Not only do your friends help shape your image but the closer they get to you, the more contact you have with them, the more it affects your identity. Peter, though vehemently denying his connection with Jesus was easily identified as one of his disciples. Even when the image suggested otherwise, he was cursing and swearing, hardly the image of Jesus and yet identified none the less. He had been sharpened by the company he kept, and as a result his identity was changed and could not be hid, no longer identified as a fisherman, but now even his speech had changed. Your image is what we see or think of you, your identity is who you are and both are affected by those closest to you.

The face expresses Intensity. If I want to determine your level of commitment, all I need do is look into your eyes. Your face will reveal your level of intensity. In sports its called "putting your game face on" if you are going to be intense you need to surround yourself with intense people. Intensity doesn't just speak of your facial expression but it speaks of your attitude or disposition in life. It's a determination, a refusal to loose or quit, you know kind of like *James 5:16 The effectual fervent prayer of a righteous man availeth much.* We must surround ourselves with people that have the right level of intensity because that intensity is contagious, and as the saying goes, "Our attitude determines our altitude." So choose your companions wisely because their attitude affects your attitude and ultimately your altitude.

Our real strength comes from God, but it is greatly affected by the people we have around us, those that have influence and authority in our lives. Let's build and establish the kingdom of God together, let's sharpen and strengthen one another. **"And finally my brethren Be strong in the Lord, and in the power of His might" Ephesians 6:10**

In conclusion, we must protect our king! As in the game of chess, so it is in life. You must protect your king at all times. The primary objective of the game of chess is to reach checkmate. Checkmate is achieved by putting the opposing player's king under immediate direct attack and threat of being captured by one or more of the player's Queen, Bishops, Knights, Rooks and/or pawns, from which the opposing King cannot escape. While chess is a game of strategy, intellect and intense concentration, its rules are simple. It has been said that the origin of the game remains lost in antiquity, but the meaning of the word chess can be traced back to Old Persian and

Arabic terms which literally mean an "**army of four divisions**". Each piece denotes a rank or division and is limited to specific moves and abilities. All have the power to kill, all have the ability to advance but not all have the ability to retreat. Some of the world's most brilliant minds are intrigued, and even fascinated with this so called game. Its appeal crosses all cultural, social, economic, academic, religious and even ethnic and racial divides. To master it, to become a champion is the dream of men of power and wealth as well as men of little means. Of all its rules, and though each piece moves autonomously and deliberately, one rule applies to all. Whether queen or pawn, rook or knight, no move is permitted that would put your King in check! That is to say; it is illegal to put the king at risk of direct attack or unavoidable escape. If we could understand and embrace this one principal, we would win far more battles than we lose. The basic rules and objectives of chess can be parabolic; they can help us understand both our liberties as well as our limitations in the kingdom. If we would adhere to but one rule; we must protect the king at all cost. The game can be won despite the loss or capture of any other piece; but once the king is exposed, the battle is over and the war has been lost. Unlike the game of chess, in life we cannot simply reset the board and play again. There are consequences, repercussions that can result in a catastrophic loss or setback. We face an enemy whose objective is to steal, kill and destroy. He doesn't follow the rules, and will stop at nothing to achieve his goal of destroying God's people. The scripture says in *1Thes 5:12-13 We beseech you, brethren, to know them which labour among you, and are over you in the Lord, and admonish you; And to esteem them very highly in love for their work's sake. And be at peace among yourselves.* We must not only know who we are, but we must properly identify those that are over us. We must properly esteem ourselves and those to whom we are connected. Whatever moves we make, whether in defense of the king or the advancement of the kingdom; always make your next move, your best move! I pray that His Kingdom comes and that His will be done in your life, as it is in heaven. I hope that something in this book has encouraged and strengthened you, and that you will become a better kingdom citizen as a result of what you have read. May God richly bless you and may His face shine upon you and may He give you peace.

*Ps 144:1 Blessed be the LORD my **strength**, which teacheth my hands to war, and my fingers to fight:*

*Ps 18:1 I will love thee, O LORD, my **strength**.*

*Ps 18:32 It is God that girdeth me with **strength**, and maketh my way perfect.*

*Ps 19:14 Let the words of my mouth, and the meditation of my heart, be acceptable in thy sight, O LORD, my **strength**, and my redeemer.*

*Ps 22:19 But be not thou far from me, O LORD: O my **strength**, haste thee to help me.*

*Ps 27:1 The LORD is my light and my salvation; whom shall I fear? the LORD is the **strength** of my life; of whom shall I be afraid?*

*Ps 46:1 God is our refuge and **strength**, a very present help in trouble.*

*Ps 73:26 My flesh and my heart faileth: but God is the **strength** of my heart, and my portion for ever.*

*Ps 144:1 Blessed be the LORD my **strength**, which teacheth my hands to war, and my fingers to fight:*

*Prov 10:29 The way of the LORD is **strength** to the upright: but destruction shall be to the workers of iniquity.*

*Prov 24:5 A wise man is strong; yea, a man of knowledge increaseth **strength.***

*Prov 24:10 If thou faint in the day of adversity, thy **strength** is small.*

*2 Cor 12:9 And he said unto me, My grace is sufficient for thee: for my **strength** is made perfect in weakness.*

*Prov 18:10 The name of the LORD is a **strong** tower: the righteous runneth into it, and is safe.*

*Joel 3:10 Beat your plowshares into swords, and your pruning-hooks into spears: let the weak say, I am **strong**.*

*Rom 15:1 We then that are **strong** ought to bear the infirmities of the weak.*

*Ps 27:14 Wait on the LORD: be of good courage, and he shall **strengthen** thine heart: wait, I say, on the LORD.*

*Ps 31:24 Be of good courage, and he shall **strengthen** your heart, all ye that hope in the LORD.*

*1 Pet 5:10 But the God of all grace, who hath called us unto his eternal glory by Christ Jesus, after that ye have suffered a while, make you perfect, establish, **strengthen**, and settle you.*

We pray that this book has blessed and encouraged you. It is our desire to inspire God's people to reach their maximum potential. For booking information, please contact.

Christ Harvest Church
2716 Interstate Street
Charlotte, NC 28208
704-399-0270

About the author,

Overseer Terry M. Clark

Graced with a unique ability to understand and explain the scripture, Overseer Clark profoundly and practically divides the word of truth. He has become a well sought after teacher in the body. He is known for his extremely passionate preaching and revelatory but relevant teaching.

Presently serving under the covering of Bishop Eric K. Clark of Cleveland, OH. Overseer Clark is the Senior Pastor of Christ Harvest Church located in Charlotte, NC.

Overseer Clark is married to Meshelle Clark, and is the proud father of two sons; Terry Mathis Clark Jr. and Devon Michael Clark.

A respected and accomplished businessman; Overseer Clark has more than twenty years experience in executive management in entertainment and hospitality industry. He is also the founder and CEO of Harvest Group Insurance and Investments. He is a community leader with community development and empowerment in mind.

Overseer Terry Mathis Clark Sr.
Christ Harvest Church
2726 Interstate St.
Charlotte, NC 28208
704-299-0270
www.chccharlotte.org
www.myspace/overseerlclark.com

CPSIA information can be obtained
at www.ICGtesting.com
Printed in the USA
FFHW022141180519
52522881-57965FF